Texts Fluency Practice

Level C

Authors

Timothy Rasinski and Lorraine Griffith

SHELL EDUCATION

3072100003225

Editor
Tracy Edmunds

Imaging
Alfred Lau

Product Director
Phil Garcia

Cover Design
Lee Aucoin

Creative Director
Lee Aucoin

Editor-in-Chief
Sharon Coan, M.S. Ed.

Publisher
Corinne Burton, M.A. Ed.

Shell Education

5301 Oceanus Drive

Huntington Beach, CA 92649-1030

www.shelleducation.com

ISBN-978-1-4258-0400-8

©2005 Shell Education

Made in U.S.A.

Reprinted, 2008

The classroom teacher may reproduce copies of materials in this book for classroom use only. The reproduction of any part for an entire school or school system is strictly prohibited. No part of this publication may be transmitted, stored, or recorded in any form without written permission from the publisher.

Table of Contents

Table of Contents *(cont.)*

Introduction

Why This Book?

We developed this book in response to teachers' needs for good texts to teach reading fluency. In the past several years, reading fluency has become recognized as an essential element in elementary and middle grade reading programs (National Reading Panel, 2001). Readers who are fluent are better able to comprehend what they read—they decode words so effortlessly that they can devote their cognitive resources to the all-important task of comprehension. Fluent readers also construct meaning by reading with appropriate expression and phrasing.

Readers develop fluency through guided practice or repeated readings—reading a text selection several times to the point where it can be expressed meaningfully, with appropriate expression and phrasing. Readers who engage in regular repeated readings, under the guidance and assistance of a teacher or other coach, improve their word recognition, reading rate, comprehension, and overall reading proficiency.

What sorts of texts lend themselves to repeated practice? To us, texts meant to be performed or read orally for an audience are ideal texts for guided repeated reading and reading fluency development. Our goal in this book has been to collect age-appropriate texts meant to be performed or read aloud by students. We have found texts that are relatively short so they can be read and reread in brief periods of time. These texts are from a variety of genres—poetry and rhymes; song lyrics; famous speeches and quotations; Reader's Theater scripts; and other texts such as jokes, cheers, and well wishes. These delightful texts are often neglected in the regular reading program that focuses largely on narrative and informational texts. The passages in this book are also part of our cultural heritage and are important parts of the cultural literacy curriculum for elementary students. Even if you are not teaching reading fluency, your students should read the texts in this book as part of their cultural heritage.

Students will find the texts in this book enjoyable and engaging. They will want to practice reading these texts because of their engaging qualities—the language patterns, the rhyme, the melody, and the inspiration they provide. They will especially want to practice the texts if you provide regular opportunities for your students to perform the texts for their classmates, parents, and other audiences.

Have fun with these texts. Read them with your students again and again. Be assured that if your students regularly read and perform the texts in this book, they will begin to develop into fluent readers who are able to decode words effortlessly and construct meaning through their oral interpretation of texts.

Introduction *(cont.)*

How to Use This Book

The texts in this book are engaging and enjoyable. Students will want to read, reread, and perform these texts. As they do, they will develop into fluent readers, improving their ability to recognize words accurately and effortlessly and reading with meaningful expression and phrasing. However, you, the teacher, are the most important part in developing instruction that uses these texts. In this section we recommend ways you can use the texts with your students.

Scheduling and Practice

The texts need to be read repeatedly over several days. We recommend you introduce one text at a time and practice it over the next three, four, or five days, depending on how quickly your students develop mastery over the text. Write the text you are going to teach on chart paper and/or put it on an overhead transparency.

Read the text with your students several times each day. Read it a few times at the beginning of each day; read it several times during various breaks in the day; and read it multiple times at the end of each day.

Make two copies of the text for each student. Have students keep one copy at school in a "fluency folder." The other copy can be sent home for students to continue practicing the text with their families. Communicate to families the importance of children continuing to practice the text at home with their parents and other family members.

Coaching Your Students

A key ingredient to repeated reading is the coaching that comes from you, the teacher. As your students practice reading the target text each week—alone, in small groups, or as an entire class—be sure to provide positive feedback about their reading. Through oral interpretation of a text readers can express joy, sadness, anger, surprise, or any of a variety of emotions. Help students learn to convey emotion and meaning in their oral reading.

You can do this by listening from time to time to students read and coaching them in the various aspects of oral interpretation. You may wish to suggest that students emphasize certain words, insert dramatic pauses, read a bit faster in one place, or slow down in other parts of the text. And, of course, lavish praise on students' best efforts to convey meaning through their reading. Although it may take a while for students to develop this sense of "voice" in their reading, in the long run it will lead to more engaged and fluent reading and higher levels of comprehension.

Introduction *(cont.)*

Word Study

Although the aim of the fluency texts in this book is to develop fluent and meaningful oral reading of texts, the practicing of passages should also provide opportunities to develop students' vocabulary and word decoding skills. Students may practice a passage repeatedly to the point where it is largely memorized. At this point, students may not look at the words in the text as closely as they should. By continually drawing attention to words in the text, you can help students maintain their focus and develop an ongoing fascination with words.

After reading a passage several times through, ask students to choose words from the passage that they think are interesting. Put these words on a word wall or ask students to add them to their personal word banks. Talk about the meaning of each word and its spelling construction. Help students develop a deepened appreciation for these words and encourage them to use these words in their oral and written language. You might, for example, ask students to use some of the chosen words in their daily journal entries.

Once a list of words has been added to your classroom word wall or students' word banks, play games with the words. One of our favorites is "word bingo." Here, students are given a card with a grid of 3 x 3, 4 x 4, or 5 x 5 boxes. In each box students randomly write a word from the word wall or bank. Then, the teacher calls out definitions of the target words or sentences that contain the target words. Students find the words on their cards and cover them with a marker. Once a horizontal, vertical, or diagonal line of words is covered, they call "Bingo" and win the game.

Have students sort the chosen words along a variety of dimensions — by number of syllables, part of speech, phonics features such as long vowel sound or a consonant blend, or by meaning (e.g, words that can express how a person can feel and words that can't). Through sorting and categorizing activities students get repeated exposure to words, all the time examining the words in different ways.

Help students expand their vocabularies with extended word family instruction. Choose a word from the texts, like "hat", and brainstorm with students other words that belong to the same word family (e.g. "cat," "bat," "chat," etc.). Once a list of family words is chosen, have students create short poems using the rhyming words. These composed poems can be used for further practice and performance. No matter how you do it, make the opportunity to examine select words from the fluency passages part of your regular instructional routine for the fluency texts. The time spent in word study will most definitely be time very well spent.

Introduction *(cont.)*

Performance

After several days of practice, arrange a special time of a day for students to perform the texts. This performance time can range from 5 minutes to 30 minutes depending on the number of texts to be read. Find a special person to listen to your children perform. You may also want to invite a neighboring class, parents, or another group to come to your room to listen to your students read. Have the children perform the targeted text as a group. Later, you can have individuals or groups of children perform the text again.

As an alternative to having your children perform for a group that comes to your room, you may want to send students to visit other adults and children in the building and perform for them. Principals, school secretaries, and visitors to the building are usually great audiences for children's reading. Tape recording and videotaping your students' reading is another way to create a performance opportunity.

Regardless of how you accomplish it, it is important that you create the opportunity for your students to perform for some audience. The magic of the performance will give students the motivation to want to practice their assigned texts.

Performance, Not Memorization

Remember, the key to developing fluency is guided reading practice. Students become more fluent when they read the text repeatedly. Reading requires students to actually see the words in the text. Thus, it is important that you do not require students to memorize the text they are practicing and performing. Memorization leads students away from the visualization of the words. Although students may want to try to memorize some texts, our instructional emphasis needs to be on reading with expression so that any audience will enjoy the students' oral rendering of the text. Keep students' eyes on the text whenever possible.

Introduction *(cont.)*

Reader's Theater

Reader's Theater is an exciting and easy method of providing students with an opportunity to practice fluency leading to a performance. Because Reader's Theater minimizes the use of props, sets, costumes, and memorization, it is an easy way to present a "play" in the classroom. Students read from a book or prepared script using their voices to bring the text to life.

Reader's Theater is a communication form that establishes contact with the audience. In traditional drama, the audience is ignored as they watch the characters perform. Reader's Theater, on the other hand, has the following characteristics:

- The script is always read and never memorized.

- Readers may be characters, narrators, or switch back and forth into various characters and parts.

- The readers may sit, stand, or both, but they do not have to perform any other actions.

- Readers use only the interpreter's tools to express emotion. These are eye contact, facial expressions, and vocal expression. The voice, especially, should be very expressive.

- Scripts may be from books, songs, poems, letters, etc. They can be performed directly from the original material or adapted specifically for the Reader's Theater performance.

- Musical accompaniment or soundtracks may be used, but are not necessary.

- Very simple props may be used, especially with younger children, to help the audience identify the parts.

Practice for the Reader's Theater should consist of coached repeated, readings that lead to a smooth, fluent presentation.

Websites and Resources for Fluency and Fluency Texts

http://www.theteachersguide.com/ChildrensSongs.htm — children's songs

http://www.niehs.nih.gov/kids/musicchild.htm — children's songs

http://www.gigglepoetry.com – fun and silly poetry

http://loiswalker.com/catalog/guidesamples.html — various scripts

http://www.ruyasonic.com/rdr_edu.htm — information on writing radio drama scripts

http://www.ruyasonic.com/at_kids.htm — information on writing radio drama scripts for children

http://www.margiepalatini.com/readerstheater.html — Reader's Theater scripts

http://www.aaronshep.com/rt/ — Reader's Theater resource

http://www.storycart.com — Reader's Theater scripts (5 free)

Note: These websites were active at the time of publication. As you know sites frequently change, so we cannot guarantee that they will always be available or at the same location.

Poetry and Rhymes

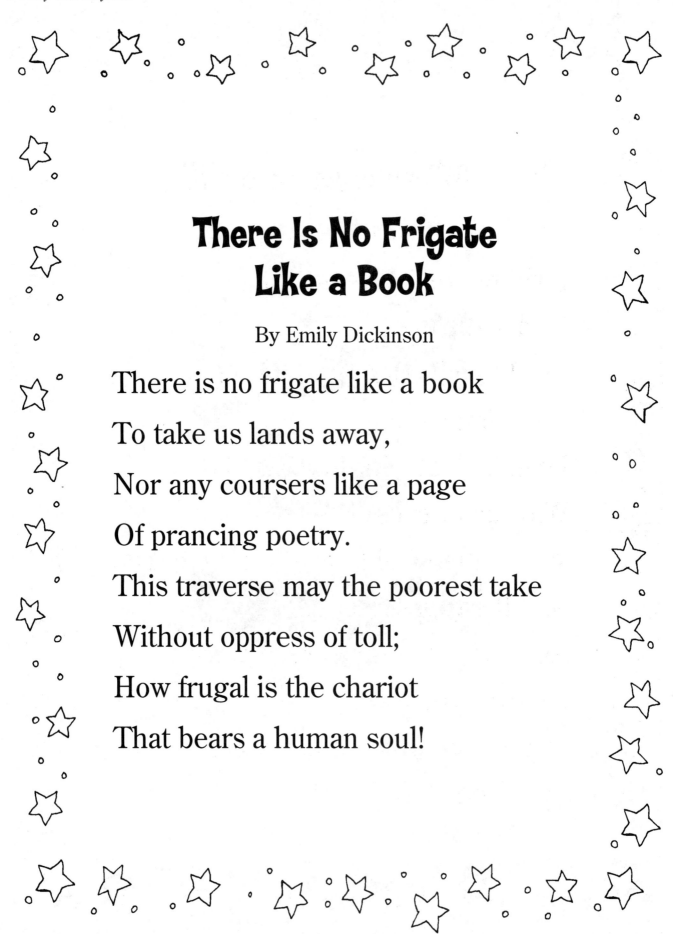

There Is No Frigate Like a Book

By Emily Dickinson

There is no frigate like a book

To take us lands away,

Nor any coursers like a page

Of prancing poetry.

This traverse may the poorest take

Without oppress of toll;

How frugal is the chariot

That bears a human soul!

Afternoon on a Hill

By Edna St. Vincent Millay

I will be the gladdest thing

Under the sun!

I will touch a hundred flowers

And not pick one.

I will look at cliffs and clouds

With quiet eyes,

Watch the wind bow down the grass,

And the grass rise.

And when lights begin to show

Up from the town,

I will mark which must be mine,

And then start down!

Clouds

By Christina Rossetti

White sheep, white sheep

On a blue hill,

When the wind stops

You all stand still,

You walk away slow.

White sheep, white sheep

Where do you go?

Fog

By Carl Sandburg

The fog comes

on little cat feet.

It sits looking

over harbor and city

on silent haunches

and then moves on.

In the Garden

By Emily Dickinson

A bird came down the walk:
He did not know I saw;
He bit an angle-worm in halves
And ate the fellow, raw.

And then he drank a dew
From a convenient grass,
And then hopped sidewise to the wall
To let a beetle pass.

He glanced with rapid eyes
That hurried all abroad,—
They looked like frightened beads, I thought;
He stirred his velvet head

Like one in danger; cautious,
I offered him a crumb,
And he unrolled his feathers
And rowed him softer home

Than oars divide the ocean,
Too silver for a seam,
Or butterflies, off banks of noon,
Leap, plashless, as they swim.

Note: *plashless* is a word!

Metamorphosis

By Kristi Bates

A poem for two voices

V1: I am a butterfly.
V2: I am a moth
Both: People think we're the same,
　　　But really we're not
V1: I spin a chrysalis.
V2: I spin a cocoon.
V1: My antennae are straight,
V2: Mine will be feathery soon.
V1: I'm awake during the day and sleep when it's night.
V2: I come out when it's dark and sleep when it's light.
V1: I rest with my wings straight up in the air.
V2: When I'm tired my wings are flat down there.
Both: Why people confuse us,
　　　We'll just never know!
　　　We're quite different creatures,
　　　As this poem does show.
V1: But wait! I think we have something the same!
V2: We do? But what it is? Stop playing this game!
V1: We both go through changes, to get where we are.
V2: You're right! Four stages will get us this far.
V1: First, we are eggs, laid in a row.
V2: Next, we are larvae, we eat and we grow.
V1: The third stage is when we are wrapped up so tight.
　　　We stay this way until we're just right.
V2: The time now has come for us to break free.
　　　We can fly up so high, as tall as a tree!
Both: We're finally together,
　　　And now we can't miss
　　　Because we've completed
　　　Metamorphosis!

The Road Not Taken

By Robert Frost

Two roads diverged in a yellow wood,
And sorry I could not travel both
And be one traveler, long I stood
And looked down one as far as I could
To where it bent in the undergrowth;
Then took the other, as just as fair,
And having perhaps the better claim,
Because it was grassy and wanted wear;
Though as for that the passing there
Had worn them really about the same,
And both that morning equally lay
In leaves no step had trodden black.
Oh, I kept the first for another day!
Yet knowing how way leads on to way,
I doubted if I should ever come back.
I shall be telling this with a sigh
Somewhere ages and ages hence:
Two roads diverged in a wood, and I—
I took the one less traveled by,
And that has made all the difference.

Theme in Yellow

By Carl Sandburg

I spot the hills
With yellow balls in autumn.
I light the prairie cornfields
Orange and tawny gold clusters
And I am called pumpkins.
On the last of October
When dusk is fallen
Children join hands
And circle round me
Singing ghost songs
And love to the harvest moon;
I am a jack-o'-lantern
With terrible teeth
And the children know
I am fooling.

This poem is performed beautifully as a monologue from the viewpoint of a pumpkin. A teacher will want to have the children read the poem as a group and several more times trying to discover who is actually the voice in this well-known poem my Sandburg.

Monday's Child Is Fair of Face

Mother Goose

Monday's child is fair of face,

Tuesday's child is full of grace,

Wednesday's child is full of woe,

Thursday's child has far to go.

Friday's child is loving and giving,

Saturday's child works hard for a living,

But the child born on the Sabbath Day,

Is fair and wise and good and gay.

Casey at the Bat

By Ernest Lawrence Thayer, 1888

The outlook wasn't brilliant for the Mudville nine that day;
The score stood four to two with but one inning more to play.
And then when Cooney died at first, and Barrows did the same,
A sickly silence fell upon the patrons of the game.
A straggling few got up to go in deep despair. The rest
Clung to that hope which springs eternal in the human breast;
They thought if only Casey could but get a whack at that
We'd put up even money now with Casey at the bat.
But Flynn preceded Casey, as did also Jimmy Blake,
And the former was a lulu and the latter was a cake;
So upon that stricken multitude grim melancholy sat,
For there seemed but little chance of Casey's getting to the bat.
But Flynn let drive a single, to the wonderment of all,
And Blake, the much despised, tore the cover off the ball;
And when the dust had lifted, and the men saw what had occurred,
There was Johnnie safe at second and Flynn a-hugging third.
Then from 5,000 throats and more there rose a lusty yell;
It rumbled through the valley, it rattled in the dell;
It knocked upon the mountain and recoiled upon the flat,
For Casey, mighty Casey, was advancing to the bat.
There was ease in Casey's manner as he stepped into his place;
There was pride in Casey's bearing and a smile on Casey's face.
And when, responding to the cheers, he lightly doffed his hat,
No stranger in the crowd could doubt 'twas Casey at the bat.
Ten thousand eyes were on him as he rubbed his hands with dirt;
Five thousand tongues applauded when he wiped them on his shirt.

Casey at the Bat *(cont.)*

Then while the writhing pitcher ground the ball into his hip,
Defiance gleamed in Casey's eye, a sneer curled Casey's lip.
And now the leather-covered sphere came hurtling through the air,
And Casey stood a-watching it in haughty grandeur there.
Close by the sturdy batsman the ball unheeded sped
"That ain't my style," said Casey. "Strike one," the umpire said.
From the benches black with people, there went up a muffled roar,
Like the beating of the storm-waves on a stern and distant shore.
"Kill him! Kill the umpire!" shouted someone on the stand;
And it's likely they'd have killed him had not Casey raised his hand.
With a smile of Christian charity great Casey's visage shone;
He stilled the rising tumult; he bade the game go on;
He signaled to the pitcher, and once more the spheroid flew;
But Casey still ignored it, and the umpire said, "Strike two."
"Fraud!" cried the maddened thousands, and echo answered fraud;
But one scornful look from Casey and the audience was awed.
They saw his face grow stern and cold, they saw his muscles strain,
And they knew that Casey wouldn't let that ball go by again.
The sneer is gone from Casey's lip, his teeth are clenched in hate;
He pounds with cruel violence his bat upon the plate.
And now the pitcher holds the ball, and now he lets it go,
And now the air is shattered by the force of Casey's blow.
Oh, somewhere in this favored land the sun is shining bright;
The band is playing somewhere, and somewhere hearts are light,
And somewhere men are laughing, and somewhere children shout;
But there is no joy in Mudville—mighty Casey has struck out.

NOTE: This poem is also available as a Reader's Theater script on page 98.

Casey's Revenge

By Grantland Rice

There were saddened hearts in Mudville for a week or even
    more;
There were muttered oaths and curses—every fan in town was
    sore.
"Just think," said one, "how soft it looked with Casey at the bat,
And then to think he'd go and spring a bush league trick like
    that!"
All his past fame was forgotten—he was now a hopeless "shine."
They called him "Strike-Out Casey," from the mayor down the
    line;
And as he came to bat each day his bosom heaved a sigh,
While a look of hopeless fury shone in mighty Casey's eye.
He pondered in the days gone by that he had been their king,
That when he strolled up to the plate they made the welkin ring;
But now his nerve had vanished, for when he heard them hoot
He "fanned" or "popped out" daily, like some minor league
    recruit.
He soon began to sulk and loaf, his batting eye went lame;
No home runs on the score card now were chalked against his
    name;
The fans without exception gave the manager no peace,
For one and all kept clamoring for Casey's quick release.
The Mudville squad began to slump, the team was in the air;
Their playing went from bad to worse—nobody seemed to care.
"Back to the woods with Casey!" was the cry from Rooters' Row.
"Get some one who can hit the ball, and let that big dub go!"

Casey's Revenge *(cont.)*

The lane is long, some one has said, that never turns again,
And Fate, though fickle, often gives another chance to men;
And Casey smiled; his rugged face no longer wore a frown—
The pitcher who had started all the trouble came to town.
All Mudville had assembled—ten thousand fans had come
To see the twirler who had put big Casey on the bum;
And when he stepped into the box, the multitude went wild;
He doffed his cap in proud disdain, but Casey only smiled.
"Play ball!" the umpire's voice rang out, and then the game
   began.
But in that throng of thousands there was not a single fan
Who thought that Mudville had a chance, and with the
   setting sun
Their hopes sank low—the rival team was leading "four to
   one."
The last half of the ninth came round, with no change in the
   score;
But when the first man up hit safe, the crowd began to roar;
The din increased, the echo of ten thousand shouts was
   heard
When the pitcher hit the second and gave "four balls" to the
   third.
Three men on base—nobody out—three runs to tie the
   game!
A triple meant the highest niche in Mudville's hall of fame;
But here the rally ended and the gloom was deep as night,
When the fourth one "fouled to catcher" and the fifth "flew
   out to right."

Casey's Revenge *(cont.)*

A dismal groan in chorus came; a scowl was on each face
When Casey walked up, bat in hand, and slowly took his place;
His bloodshot eyes in fury gleamed, his teeth were clenched in
    hate;
He gave his cap a vicious hook and pounded on the plate.
But fame is fleeting as the wind and glory fades away;
There were no wild and woolly cheers, no glad acclaim this day;
They hissed and groaned and hooted as they clamored:
    "Strike him out!"
But Casey gave no outward sign that he had heard this shout.
The pitcher smiled and cut one loose—across the plate it sped;
Another hiss, another groan. "Strike one!" the umpire said.
Zip! Like a shot the second curve broke just below the knee.
"Strike two!" the umpire roared aloud; but Casey made no plea.
No roasting for the umpire now—his was an easy lot;
But here the pitcher whirled again—was that a rifle shot?
A whack, a crack, and out through the space the leather pellet
    flew,
A blot against the distant sky, a speck against the blue.
Above the fence in center field in rapid whirling flight
The sphere sailed on—the blot grew dim and then was lost to
    sight.
Ten thousand hats were thrown in air, ten thousand threw a fit,
But no one ever found the ball that mighty Casey hit.
O, somewhere in this favored land dark clouds may hide the
    sun,
And somewhere bands no longer play and children have no fun!
And somewhere over blighted lives there hangs a heavy pall,
But Mudville hearts are happy now, for Casey hit the ball.

The Pobble Who Has No Toes

By Edward Lear

The Pobble who has no toes
Had once as many as we;
When they said, "Some day you may lose them all,"—
He replied, "Fish fiddle de-dee!"
And his Aunt Jobiska made him drink
Lavender water tinged with pink;
For she said, "The World in general knows
There's nothing so good for a Pobble's toes!"

The Pobble who has no toes
Swam across the Bristol Channel;
But before he set out he wrapped his nose
In a piece of scarlet flannel.
For his Aunt Jobiska said, "No harm
Can come to his toes if his nose is warm;
And it's perfectly known that a Pobble's toes
Are safe provided he minds his nose."

The Pobble swam fast and well,
And when boats or ships came near him,
He tinkledy-blinkledy-winkled a bell
So that all the world could hear him.
And all the Sailors and Admirals cried,
When they saw him nearing the farther side,
"He has gone to fish for his Aunt Jobiska's
Runcible Cat with crimson whiskers!"

The Pobble Who Has No Toes *(cont.)*

But before he touched the shore
The shore of the Bristol Channel,
A sea-green Porpoise carried away
His wrapper of scarlet flannel.
And when he came to observe his feet,
Formerly garnished with toes so neat,
His face at once became forlorn
On perceiving that all his toes were gone!

And nobody ever knew,
From that dark day to the present,
Whoso had taken the Pobble's toes,
In a manner so far from pleasant.
Whether the shrimps or crawfish gray,
Or crafty mermaids stole them away,
Nobody knew; and nobody knows
How the Pobble was robbed of his twice five toes!

The Pobble who has no toes
Was placed in a friendly Bark,
And they rowed him back and carried him up
To his Aunt Jobiska's Park.
And she made him a feast at his earnest wish,
Of eggs and buttercups fried with fish;
And she said, "It's a fact the whole world knows,
That Pobbles are happier without their toes."

Limericks

By Edward Lear

There was an Old Man who forgot
That his tea was excessively hot
When they said, "Let it cool,"
He answered, "You fool!
I shall pour it back into the pot."

There was an Old Man in a tree,
Who was horribly bored by a bee.
When they said, "Does it buzz?"
He replied, "Yes, it does!
It's a regular brute of a bee!"

There was an Old Man in a tree,
Whose whiskers were lovely to see;
But the birds of the air
Pluck'd them perfectly bare
To make themselves nests in that tree.

There was an Old Person whose habits
Induced him to feed upon rabbits;
When he'd eated eighteen,
He turned perfectly green,
Upon which he relinquished those habits.

Mr. Nobody

Author Unknown

I know a funny little man,
As quiet as a mouse,
Who does the mischief that is done
In everybody's house!
There's no one ever sees his face,
And yet we all agree
That every plate we break was cracked
By Mr. Nobody.

'Tis he who always tears our books,
Who leaves the door ajar,
He pulls the buttons from our shirts,
And scatters pins afar;
That squeaking door will always squeak,
For, Friend, don't you see,
We leave the oiling to be done
By Mr. Nobody.

He puts damp wood upon the fire,
That kettles cannot boil;
His are the feet that bring in the mud,
And all the carpets soil.
The papers always are mislaid,
Who had them last but he?
There's not one tosses them about
But Mr. Nobody.

The finger marks upon the door
By none of us are made;
We never leave the blinds unclosed,
To let the curtains fade;
The ink we never spill; the boots
That lying around you see
Are not our boots; they all belong
To Mr. Nobody!

Jabberwocky

By Lewis Carroll

'Twas brillig, and the slithy toves
Did gyre and gimble in the wabe:
All mimsy were the borogoves,
And the mome raths outgrabe.

"Beware the Jabberwock, my son!
The jaws that bite, the claws that catch!
Beware the Jubjub bird, and shun
The frumious Bandersnatch!"

He took his vorpal sword in hand:
Long time the manxome foe he sought
So rested he by the Tumtum tree,
And stood awhile in thought.

And, as in uffish thought he stood,
The Jabberwock, with eyes of flame,
Came whiffling through the tulgey wood,
And burbled as it came!

One, two! One, two! And through and through
The vorpal blade went snicker-snack!
He left it dead, and with its head
He went galumphing back.

"And, has thou slain the Jabberwock?
Come to my arms, my beamish boy!
O frabjous day! Callooh! Callay!"
He chortled in his joy.

'Twas brillig, and the slithy toves
Did gyre and gimble in the wabe;
All mimsy were the borogoves,
And the mome raths outgrabe.

Three-Dimensional Shapes

By Lorraine Griffith

Sphere
It's perfectly round
A globe
The whole ball of wax
Spherical

Cone
It's pointy and flat
A Dixie cup
Ice Cream you scream, we all scream for ice cream!
Conical

Cylinder
Straight sides with circular ends of equal size
A toilet paper tube
Please don't squeeze the Charmin!
Cylindrical

Pyramid
It's a square base with a vertex
A royal tomb in Ancient Egypt
Stay clear of pyramid schemes!
Pyramidal

Cube
A hexahedron, six square faces
A perfectly squared box
As cool as an ice cube
Cubical

Rectangular prism
A square base with rectangular sides
A box of foil or plastic wrap
Don't box me in!
Prismatical

NOTE: Learning the names and characteristics of 3-D shapes has been difficult for some of my math students. Incorporating descriptions and examples of each vocabulary word has helped them to master the names of the shapes.

O Captain! My Captain!

By Walt Whitman

O Captain! my Captain! our fearful trip is done,
The ship has weather'd every rack, the prize we sought is won,
The port is near, the bells I hear, the people all exulting,
While follow eyes the steady keel, the vessel grim and daring;
    But O heart! heart! heart!
      O the bleeding drops of red,
        Where on the deck my Captain lies,
          Fallen cold and dead.

O Captain! my Captain! rise up and hear the bells;
Rise up for you the flag is flung for you the bugle trills,
For you bouquets and ribbon'd wreaths for you the shores a-
    crowding,
For you they call, the swaying mass, their eager faces turning;
    Here Captain! dear father!
      This arm beneath your head!
        It is some dream that on the deck,
          You've fallen cold and dead.

My Captain does not answer, his lips are pale and still,
My father does not feel my arm, he has no pulse nor will,
The ship is anchor'd safe and sound, its voyage closed and done,
From fearful trip the victor ship comes in with object won;
    Exult O shores, and ring O bells!
    But I with mournful tread,
      Walk the deck my Captain lies,
        Fallen cold and dead.

Although never mentioned by name, Abraham Lincoln is the subject of Walt Whitman's famous poem. Lincoln was assassinated on April 14, 1865, less than a week after the Civil War had ended.

In Flanders Fields

By John McCrae

In Flanders fields the poppies blow
Between the crosses, row on row
That mark our place; and in the sky
The larks, still bravely singing, fly
Scarce heard amid the guns below.

We are the Dead. Short days ago
We lived, felt dawn, saw sunset glow,
Loved and were loved, and now we lie
   In Flanders fields.

Take up our quarrel with the foe:
To you from failing hands we throw
The torch; be yours to hold it high.
If ye break faith with us who die
We shall not sleep, though poppies grow
   In Flanders fields.

What If the Score Is Against You?

Author Unknown

What if the score is against you,

And you know defeat is sure?

Keep giving your best

Defeat is a test

To see if you can endure.

Come in on your feet at life's ending,

And the past will feel full and fine.

There's a healthy glow

Only doers can know,

In the sprint at the finish line.

 ©Shell Educational Publishing

Song Lyrics

Waltzing Matilda

By A. B. (Banjo) Paterson

Once a jolly swagman camped by a Billabong
Under the shade of a Coolabah tree
And he sang as he watched and waited till his billy boiled,
"Who'll come a-waltzing Matilda with me?"

Down come a jumbuck to drink at the water hole
Up jumped a swagman and grabbed him in glee
And he sang as he stowed him away in his tucker bag,
"You'll come a-waltzing Matilda with me."

Up rode the Squatter a riding his thoroughbred
Up rode the Trooper—one, two, three
"Where's that jumbuck you've got in your tucker bag?"
"You'll come a-waltzing Matilda with me."

But the swagman he up and jumped in the water hole
Drowning himself by the Coolabah tree,
And his ghost may be heard as it sings in the Billabong,
"Who'll come a-waltzing Matilda with me?"

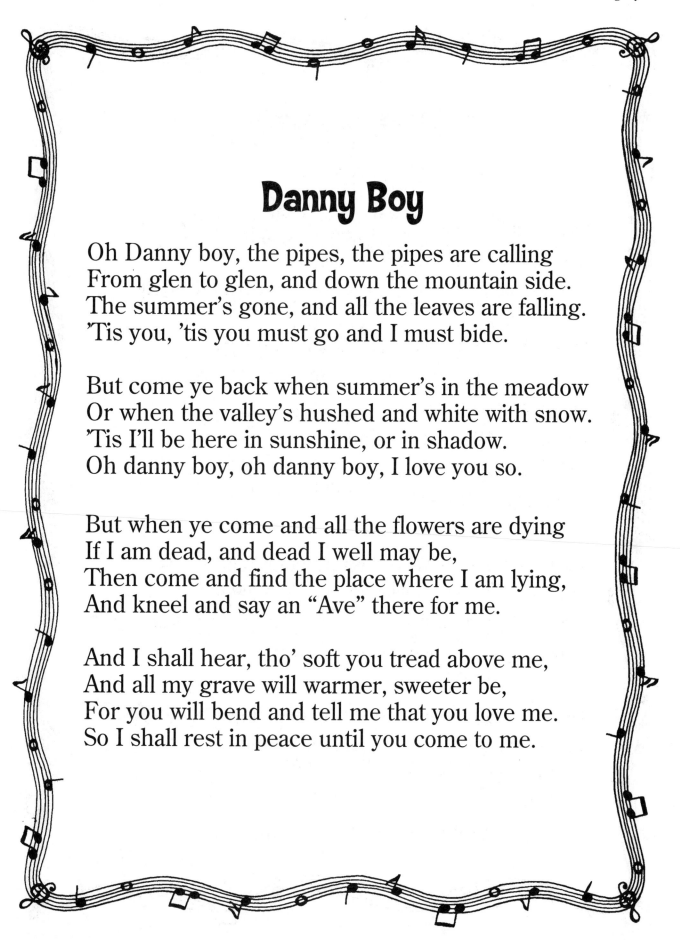

Danny Boy

Oh Danny boy, the pipes, the pipes are calling
From glen to glen, and down the mountain side.
The summer's gone, and all the leaves are falling.
'Tis you, 'tis you must go and I must bide.

But come ye back when summer's in the meadow
Or when the valley's hushed and white with snow.
'Tis I'll be here in sunshine, or in shadow.
Oh danny boy, oh danny boy, I love you so.

But when ye come and all the flowers are dying
If I am dead, and dead I well may be,
Then come and find the place where I am lying,
And kneel and say an "Ave" there for me.

And I shall hear, tho' soft you tread above me,
And all my grave will warmer, sweeter be,
For you will bend and tell me that you love me.
So I shall rest in peace until you come to me.

Greensleeves

Alas, my love, you do me wrong,
To cast me off discourteously.
For I have loved you well and long,
Delighting in your company.

Chorus:
Greensleeves was all my joy
Greensleeves was my delight,
Greensleeves was my heart of gold,
And who but my lady greensleeves.

Your vows you've broken, like my heart,
Oh, why did you so enrapture me?
Now I remain in a world apart
But my heart remains in captivity.

Chorus

I have been ready at your hand,
To grant whatever you would crave,
I have both wagered life and land,
Your love and good-will for to have.

Chorus

If you intend thus to disdain,
It does the more enrapture me,
And even so, I still remain
A lover in captivity.

Chorus

Greensleeves *(cont.)*

My men were clothed all in green,
And they did ever wait on thee;
All this was gallant to be seen,
And yet thou wouldst not love me.

Chorus

Thou couldst desire no earthly thing,
But still thou hadst it readily.
Thy music still to play and sing;
And yet thou wouldst not love me.

Chorus

Well, I will pray to God on high,
That thou my constancy mayst see,
And that yet once before I die,
Thou wilt vouchsafe to love me.

Chorus

Ah, Greensleeves, now farewell, adieu,
To God I pray to prosper thee,
For I am still thy lover true,
Come once again and love me.

Chorus

The Yellow Rose of Texas

There's a yellow rose in Texas, that I am going to see,
Nobody else could miss her, not half as much as me.
She cried so when I left her, it like to broke my heart,
And if I ever find her, we nevermore will part.

Chorus:
She's the sweetest little rosebud that Texas ever knew,
Her eyes are bright as diamonds, they sparkle like the dew;
You may talk about your Clementine, and sing of Rosalee,
But the yellow rose of Texas is the only girl for me.

Chorus

When the Rio Grande is flowing, the starry skies are bright,
She walks along the river in the quiet summer night:
I know that she remembers, when we parted long ago,
I promise to return again, and not to leave her so.

Chorus

Oh now I'm going to find her, for my heart is full of woe,
And we'll sing the songs together, that we sung so long ago
We'll play the bango gaily, and we'll sing the songs of yore,
And the yellow rose of Texas shall be mine forevermore.

Chorus

Red River Valley

From this valley they say you are going,
We will miss your bright eyes and sweet smile,
For they say you are taking the sunshine
That has brightened our path for a while.

Come and sit by my side if you love me,
Do not hasten to bid me adieu,
But remember the Red River Valley
And the cowboy who loved you so true.

Won't you think of the valley you're leaving?
Oh how lonely, how sad it will be.
Oh think of the fond heart you're breaking,
And the grief you are causing to me.

As you go to your home by the ocean,
May you never forget those sweet hours,
That we spent in the Red River Valley,
And the love we exchanged 'mid the flowers.

Oh Shenandoah

Oh, Shenandoah, I long to hear you.
Look away, you rollin' river.
Oh, Shenandoah, I long to hear you.
Look away. We're bound away.
Across the wide Missouri.

Now the Missouri is a mighty river.
Look away, you rollin' river.
Indians camp along her border.
Look away. We're bound away
Across the wide Missouri.

Well a white man loved an Indian maiden.
Look away, you rollin' river.
With notions his canoe was laden.
Look away, we're bound away
Across the wide Missouri.

Oh Shenandoah, I love your daughter.
Look away, you rollin' river.
It was for her I'd cross the water.
Look away, we're bound away
Across the wide Missouri.

For seven long years I courted Sally.
Look away, you rollin' river.
Seven more years I longed to have her.
Look away, we're bound away
Across the wide Missouri.

Well, it's fare-thee-well, my dear,
I'm bound to leave you
Look away you rollin' river
Shenandoah, I will not deceive you
Look away, we're bound away
Across the wide Missouri.

Sweet Betsy from Pike

Did you ever hear of
Sweet Betsy from Pike,
Who crossed the wide prairies
With her husband, Ike,
With two yoke of cattle
And one spotted hog
A tall Shanghai rooster
And an old yeller dog?

Sing toorali, oorali, oorali ay
Sing toorali, oorali, oorali ay

The alkali desert
Was burning and bare
And Ike cried in fear,
"We are lost, I declare!
My dear old Pike County,
I'll go back to you."
Said Betsy, "You'll go by yourself,
If you do."

Sing toorali, oorali, oorali ay
Sing toorali, oorali, oorali ay

They swam the wide rivers
And crossed the tall peaks
They camped on the prairie
For weeks upon weeks
They fought off the Indians
With musket and ball
And reached California
In spite of it all.

Sing toorali, oorali, oorali ay
Sing toorali, oorali, oorali ay

By the Beautiful Sea

By Harold Atteridge

By the sea, by the sea, by the beautiful sea,

You and I, you and I, oh how happy we'll be.

When each wave comes 'a rolling in

We will duck or swim, and we'll float and fool around the water.

Over and under and then up for air.

Pa is rich, Ma is rich, so now what do we care?

I love to be beside your side, beside the sea,

Beside the seaside, by the beautiful sea.

The Caisson Song

Over hill, over dale
As we hit the dusty trail,
And the caissons go rolling along.
In and out, hear them shout,
Counter march and right about,
And the caissons go rolling along.
Then it's hi! hi! hee!
In the field artillery,
Shout out your numbers loud and strong,
For where e'er you go,
You will always know
That the caissons go rolling along. In the
storm, in the night,
Action left or action right
See those caissons go rolling along
Limber front, limber rear,
Prepare to mount your cannoneer
And those caissons go rolling along.
Then it's hi! hi! hee!
In the field artillery,
Shout out your numbers loud and strong,
For where e'er you go,
You will always know
That the caissons go rolling along.

The Battle Hymn of the Republic

By Julia Ward Howe

Mine eyes have seen the glory of the coming of the Lord
He is trampling out the vintage where the grapes of wrath are stored,
He has loosed the fateful lightening of His terrible swift sword
His truth is marching on.
    Glory! Glory! Hallelujah!
    Glory! Glory! Hallelujah!
    Glory! Glory! Hallelujah!
    His truth is marching on.

I have seen Him in the watch-fires of a hundred circling camps
They have builded Him an altar in the evening dews and damps
I can read His righteous sentence by the dim and flaring lamps
His day is marching on.
    Glory! Glory! Hallelujah!
    Glory! Glory! Hallelujah!
    Glory! Glory! Hallelujah!
    His truth is marching on.

I have read a fiery gospel writ in burnish 'd rows of steel,
"As ye deal with my contemners, So with you my grace shall deal;"
Let the Hero, born of woman, crush the serpent with his heel
Since God is marching on.
    Glory! Glory! Hallelujah!
    Glory! Glory! Hallelujah!
    Glory! Glory! Hallelujah!
    His truth is marching on.

He has sounded forth the trumpet that shall never call retreat
He is sifting out the hearts of men before His judgment-seat
Oh, be swift, my soul, to answer Him! be jubilant, my feet!
Our God is marching on.
    Glory! Glory! Hallelujah!
    Glory! Glory! Hallelujah!
    Glory! Glory! Hallelujah!
    His truth is marching on.

In the beauty of the lilies Christ was born across the sea,
With a glory in His bosom that transfigures you and me:
As He died to make men holy, let us die to make men free,
While God is marching on.
    Glory! Glory! Hallelujah!
    Glory! Glory! Hallelujah!
    Glory! Glory! Hallelujah!
    His truth is marching on.

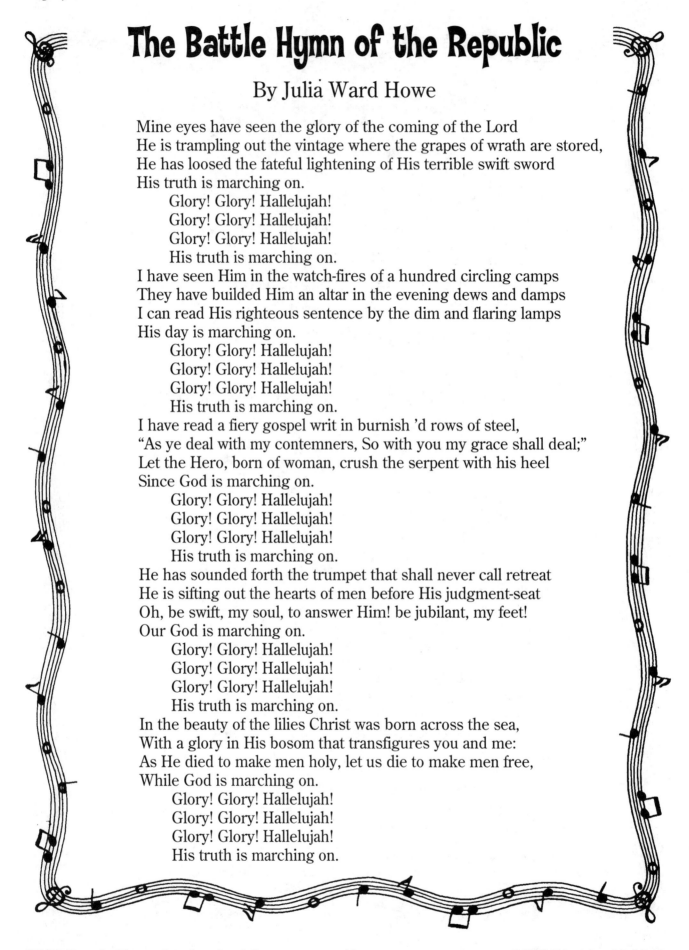

I Heard the Bells on Christmas Day

By Henry Wadsworth Longfellow

I heard the bells on Christmas day
Their old familiar carols play,
And wild and sweet the words repeat
Of peace on earth, good will to men.

And thought how, as the day had come,
The belfries of all Christendom
Had rolled along the unbroken song
Of peace on earth, good will to men.

And in despair I bowed my head
"There is no peace on earth," I said,
"For hate is strong and mocks the song
Of peace on earth, good will to men."

Then pealed the bells more loud and deep:
"God is not dead, nor doth He sleep;
The wrong shall fail, the right prevail
With peace on earth, good will to men."

Till ringing, singing on its way
The world revolved from night to day,
A voice, a chime, a chant sublime
Of peace on earth, good will to men.

Then from each black, accursed mouth
The cannon thundered in the South,
And with the sound the carols drowned
Of peace on earth, good will to men.

It was as if an earthquake rent
The hearth-stones of a continent,
And made forlorn, the households born
Of peace on earth, good will to men.

NOTE: This hymn was written during the American Civil War, as reflected by the sense of despair in the next to last stanza. Stanzas 6-7 speak of the battle, and are usually omitted.

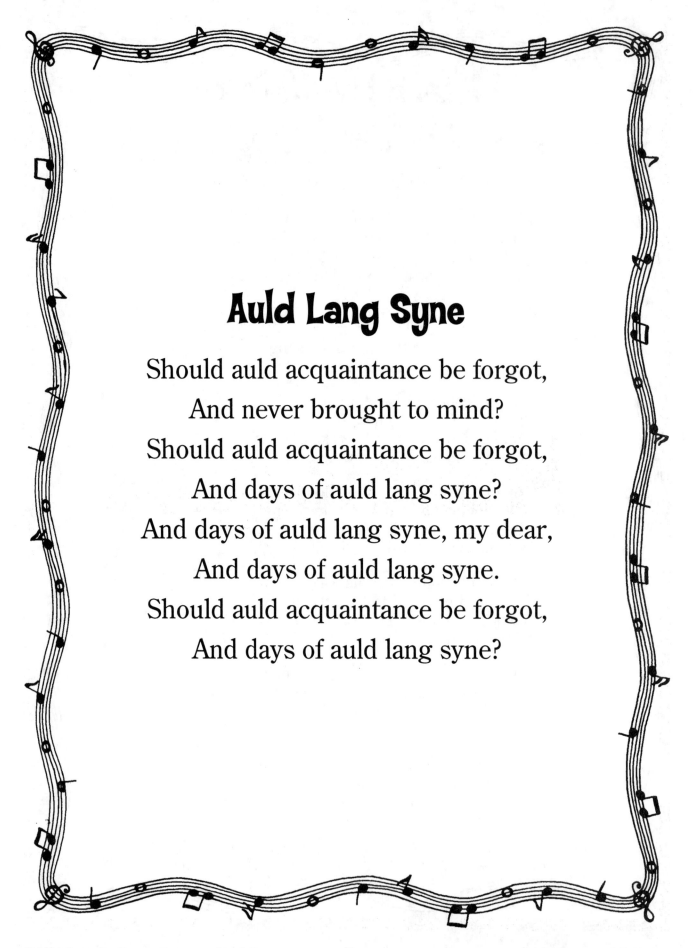

Auld Lang Syne

Should auld acquaintance be forgot,

And never brought to mind?

Should auld acquaintance be forgot,

And days of auld lang syne?

And days of auld lang syne, my dear,

And days of auld lang syne.

Should auld acquaintance be forgot,

And days of auld lang syne?

Monologues

Tecumseh: I Am a Shawnee

Tecumseh was a chief of the Shawnee Indians who was born about 1768. On August 12th, in 1810, Tecumseh delivered this speech before William Henry Harrison when he was governor of Indiana Territory. While Tecumseh had been away, large tracks of land on both sides of the Wabash River had been sold by the Indians.

It is true I am a Shawnee. My forefathers were warriors. Their son is a warrior. From them I take only my existence; from my tribe I take nothing. I am the maker of my own fortune; and oh! that I could make of my own fortune; and oh! that I could make that of my red people, and of my country, as great as the conceptions of my mind, when I think of the Spirit that rules the universe. I would not then come to Governor Harrison to ask him to tear the treaty and to obliterate the landmark; but I would say to him: "Sir, you have liberty to return to your own country."

The being within, communing with past ages, tells me that once, nor until lately, there was no white man on this continent; that it then all belonged to red men, children of the same parents, placed on it by the Great Spirit that made them, to keep it, to traverse it, to enjoy its productions, and to fill it with the same race, once a happy race, since made miserable by the white people, who are never contented but always encroaching. The way, and the only way, to check and to stop this evil, is for all the red men to unite in claiming a common and equal right in the land, as it was at first, and should be yet; for it never was divided, but belongs to all for the use of each. For no part has a right to sell, even to each other, much less to strangers—those who want all, and will not do with less.

The white people have no right to take the land from the Indians, because they had it first; it is theirs. They may sell, but all must join. Any sale not made by all is not valid. The late sale is bad. It was made by a part only. Part do not know how to sell. All red men have equal rights to the unoccupied land. The right of occupancy is as good in one place as in another. There can not be two occupations in the same place. The first excludes all others. It is not so in hunting or traveling; for there the same ground will serve many, as they may follow each other all day; but the camp is stationary, and that is occupancy. It belongs to the first who sits down on his blanket or skins which he has thrown upon the ground; and till he leaves it no other has a right.

A New Yorker Visits the Appalachians

This is an old piece of writing by a New Yorker by the name of Olmstead who visited the Appalachian Mountains in 1860. His description of the beautiful mountain setting and the people who lived there gives us a piece of history first hand. The journal entry begins with Mr. Olmstead looking for a place to stay the night as he traveled through the mountains.

At night...to find a house at which my horse could be suitably fed. . . I followed a cart path up a pretty brook in a mountain glen, till I came to an irregular-shaped cattle yard in the midst of which was a rather picturesque cabin, the roof being secured by logs laid across it and held in place by long upright pins. . .

An old man and his wife, with one hired man, were the occupants; they had come to this place from North Carolina two years before. They were very good, simple people; social and talkative, but at frequent intervals the old man, often in the midst of conversation...would groan aloud and sigh out, 'Glory to God!' or 'Oh, my blessed Lord!' or 'Lord, have mercy on us!'. . . and the woman would respond with a groan. . .

They talked with great geniality and kindness, however, and learning that I was from New York said that I had reminded them, 'by the way I talked,' of some New York people who had moved near to where they had lived in North Carolina and whom they seemed to have much liked.

'They was well larned people,' the old man said; 'though they warn't rich, they was as well larned as any, but they was the most friendly people I ever see. Most of our country folks, when they is well larned, is too proud, they won't hardly speak civil to the common; but these Yorkers wasn't so the least bit; they was the civilest people I ever seed. When I see the gals coming over to our housen, I nat'rally rejoiced; they always made it so pleasant. I never see no people who could talk so well.'

He and his wife frequently referred to them afterwards, and complimented me by saying that 'they should have know me for a Yorker by my speeching so much like them.' (1860, Olmsted, pp. 266-267)

NOTE: I used a whole collection of these mountaineer journal excerpts for a unit on Appalachia. The students in my North Carolina classroom, thought it was very funny hearing the mispronunciation of words and the New Yorker's take on the language. One girl in my room had the class in stitches as she bellowed, "They was well larned people!" http://www.wncheritage.org/

Company 'Aytch (H)

Reader mine, did you live in that stormy period?

In the year of our Lord eighteen hundred and sixty-one, do you remember those trying times?

Do you recollect in that year, for the first time in your life, of hearing Dixie and the Bonnie Blue Flag?

Fort Sumter was fired upon from Charleston by troops under General Beauregard, and Major Anderson, of the Federal army, surrendered. The die was cast; war was declared. Lincoln called for troops from Tennessee and all the Southern states, but Tennessee, loyal to Southern sister states passed the ordinance of secession, and enlisted under the Stars and Bars.

From that day on every person, almost, was eager for war, and we were all afraid it would be over and we not in the fight. Companies were made up, regiments organized; left, left, left, was heard from morning till night. By the right flank, file left march, were familiar sounds. Everywhere could be seen Southern stockades made by the ladies and our sweethearts. And some who afterwards became Union men made the most fiery secession speeches.

Flags made by the ladies were presented to companies, and to hear the young orators tell of how they would protect that flag, and that they would come back with the flag or come not at all, and if they fell they would fall with their backs to the field and their feet to the foe, would fairly make our hair stand on end with intense patriotism, and we wanted to march right off and whip twenty Yankees.

But we soon found out that the glory of war was at home among the ladies and not upon the field of blood and carnage of death, where our comrades were mutilated and torn by shot and shell. And to see the cheek blanch and to hear the fervent prayer, aye, I might say the agony of mind were very different indeed from the patriotic times at home.

NOTE: This journal entry would go very well with Walt Whitman's "Drum Taps" during a study of the Civil War. The whole contrast of patriotism before joining the war and the reality of the war itself seems to come through in both pieces.

So Then to Every Man

Thomas Wolfe

So then to every man his chance — to every man,
regardless of his birth, his shining golden opportunity
— to every man the right to live, to work, to be himself
and to become whatever thing his manhood and his
vision make him — this, seeker, is the promise of
America.

NOTE: A number of years ago, I became intrigued with the idea of a class motto to focus attention on a child's potential and my own responsibility as a teacher molding a child's character during my short year with them. My husband, a huge Thomas Wolfe fan, found this quote for me. I have loved using it with my class. It has integrated into many units we have studied, particularly civil rights and history classes. It also applies to classroom situations, playground arguments, and graduations. What I wanted most for my students, was a vision for their lives that valued work and their individual gifts. We read this together every afternoon of fourth grade, eventually memorizing the text.

Although the text is written for "man," one could easily change the text to "to everyone his chance" and lessen the gender specific language.

The Luckiest Man on the Face of the Earth

By Lou Gehrig

New York City, July 4, 1939

Fans, for the past two weeks you have been reading about a bad break I got. Yet today I consider myself the luckiest man on the face of the earth. I have been in ballparks for 17 years and have never received anything but kindness and encouragement from you fans. Look at these grand men. Which of you wouldn't consider it the highlight of his career just to associate with them for even one day?

Sure I'm lucky. Who wouldn't consider it an honor to have known Jacob Ruppert; also the builder of baseball's greatest empire, Ed Barrow; to have spent six years with that wonderful little fellow Miller Huggins; then to have spent the next nine years with that outstanding leader, that smart student of psychology—the best manager in baseball today—Joe McCarthy!

Sure I'm lucky. When the New York Giants, a team you would give your right arm to beat, and vice versa, sends you a gift, that's something! When everybody down to the groundskeepers and those boys in white coats remember you with trophies, that's something.

When you have a wonderful mother-in-law who takes sides with you in squabbles against her own daughter, that's something. When you have a father and mother who work all their lives so that you can have an education and build your body, it's a blessing! When you have a wife who has been a tower of strength and shown more courage than you dreamed existed, that's the finest I know.

So I close in saying that I might have had a tough break; but I have an awful lot to live for!

This is a piece that goes well with courage in a unit on character. I used this speech in a unit during the spring with Cal Ripkin's Reader's Theater and Casey at the Bat. Knowing some of what Lou Gehrig was suffering with will help the students to appreciate his positive outlook on life during this speech.

Reader's Theater Scripts

Paul Revere's Ride

By Henry Wadsworth Longfellow

A Reader's Theater for a whole class: 27 parts. Note that the lines marked "All" should be said in a whisper while the readers are saying their lines in full voice.

All: Shhhhhhhhhhhhhhhh
Listen, listen, listen
Listen my children
Listen, listen, listen
Listen my children and you shall hear
One if by land, two if by sea

Reader 1:   Listen, my children and you shall hear
Of the midnight ride of Paul Revere,
On the eighteenth of April, in Seventy-five;
Hardly a man is now alive
Who remembers that famous day and year.

All: Listen, listen, listen

Reader 2:   He said to his friend, "If the British march
By land or sea from the town tonight,
Hang a lantern aloft in the belfry arch
Of the North Church tower as a signal light,

Reader 3:   One, if by land, and two, if by sea;

All: One if by land, two if by sea,
One if by land two if by sea,

Reader 3:   And I on the opposite shore will be,
Ready to ride and spread the alarm
Through every Middlesex village and farm,
For the country folk to be up and to arm."

All: Listen, listen, listen

Reader 4:   Then he said, "Good night!" and with muffled oar
Silently rowed to the Charlestown shore,
Just as the moon rose over the bay,
Where swinging wide at her moorings lay

Paul Revere's Ride *(cont.)*

Reader 5: The *Somerset*, British man-of-war;
A phantom ship, with each mast and spar
Across the moon like a prison bar,
And a huge black hulk, that was magnified
By its own reflection in the tide.

All: Listen, listen, listen

Reader 6: Meanwhile, his friend, through alley and street
Wanders and watches with eager ears,
Till in the silence around him he hears

Reader 7: The muster of men at the barrack door,
The sound of arms, and the tramp of feet,
And the measured tread of the grenadiers,
Marching down to their boats on the shore.

All: Listen, listen, listen
Listen my children
Listen, listen, listen
Listen my children and you shall hear
One if by land, two if by sea

Reader 7: Then he climbed the tower of the Old North Church,
By the wooden stairs with stealthy tread,
To the belfry chamber over head,
And startled the pigeons from their perch

Reader 8: On the somber rafters, that 'round him made
Masses and moving shapes of shade ,—
By the trembling ladder, steep and tall,
To the highest window in the wall,
Where he paused to listen and look down
A moment on the roofs of the town
And the moonlight flowing over all.

Paul Revere's Ride *(cont.)*

All: Listen, listen, listen

Reader 9: Beneath, in the churchyard, lay the dead,
In their night-encampment on the hill,
Wrapped in silence so deep and still
That he could hear, like a sentinel's tread,
The watchful night-wind, as it went
Creeping along from tent to tent,
And seeming to whisper,

All: "All is well!" (whispered)

Reader 10: A moment only he feels the spell
Of the place and the hour and the secret dread
Of the lonely belfry and the dead;
For suddenly all his thoughts are bent
On a shadowy something far away,

Reader 11: Where the river widens to meet the bay,
A line of black that bends and floats
On the rising tide, like a bridge of boats.
Meanwhile, impatient to mount and ride,
Booted and spurred, with a heavy stride
On the opposite shore walked Paul Revere.

All: Listen, listen, listen
Listen my children
Listen, listen, listen
Listen my children and you shall hear
One if by land, two if by sea

Reader 12: Now he patted his horse's side,
Now gazed at the landscape far and near,
Then impetuous, stamped the earth
And turned and tightened his saddle-girth;

Reader 13: But mostly he watched with eager search
The belfry-tower of the Old North Church,
As it rose above the graves on the hill,
Lonely and spectral and somber and still.

Paul Revere's Ride *(cont.)*

Reader 14: And lo! as he looks, on the belfry's height
A glimmer, and then a gleam of light:
He springs to the saddle, the bridle he turns,
But lingers and gazes, Till full on his sight
A second lamp in the belfry burns!

All: Listen, listen, listen
Listen my children
One if by land, two if by sea
Listen, listen, listen
One if by land, two if by sea
Listen my children and you shall hear
One if by land, two if by sea

Reader 15: A hurry of hoofs in a village street,
A shape in the moonlight, a bulk in the dark,
And beneath, from the pebbles, in passing a spark
Struck out by a steed flying fearless and fleet;

All: That was all!

Reader 16: And yet, through the gloom and the light,
The fate of a nation was riding that night;
And the spark struck out by that steed in his flight,
Kindled the land into flame with its heat.

Reader 17: He has left the village and mounted the steep,
And beneath him, tranquil and broad and deep,
Is the *Mystic*, meeting the ocean tides;

Reader 18: And under the alders, that skirt its edge,
Now soft on the sand now loud on the ledge
Is heard the tramp of his steed as he rides.

Reader 19: It was twelve by the village clock
When he crossed the bridge into Medford town.
He heard the crowing of the cock,
And the barking of the farmer's dog,
And felt the damp of the river fog,
That rises after the sun goes down.

Paul Revere's Ride *(cont.)*

All: Listen, listen, listen
Listen my children
Regulars are coming, regulars

Reader 20: It was one by the village clock,
When he galloped into Lexington.
He saw the gilded weathercock
Swim in the moonlight as he passed,

Reader 21: And the meeting-house windows, blank and bare,
Gaze at him with a spectral glare,
As if they already stood aghast
At the bloody work they would look upon.

All: Listen, listen, listen
Listen my children
Regulars are coming, regulars

Reader 22: It was two by the village clock,
When he came to the bridge in Concord town.
He heard the bleating of the flock,
And the twitter of birds among the trees,
And felt the breath of the morning breeze
Blowing over the meadows brown.

Reader 23: And one was safe and asleep in his bed
Who at the bridge would be first to fall,
Who at the bridge would be lying dead,
Pierced by a British musket-ball.

All: Listen, listen, listen
Listen my children
Regulars are coming, regulars

Reader 24: You know the rest. In the books you have read,
How the British Regulars fired and fled,—

Reader 25: How the farmers gave them ball for ball,
From behind each fence and farmyard wall,
Chasing the redcoats down the lane,
Then crossing the fields to emerge again
Under the trees at the turn of the road.
And only pausing to fire and load.

Paul Revere's Ride *(cont.)*

Readers 1-5: So through the night rode Paul Revere;

Readers 1-10: And so through the night went his cry of alarm

Readers 1-15: To every Middlesex village and farm,—
A cry of defiance, and not of fear,

Readers 1-20: A voice in the darkness, a knock at the door,

Readers 1-25: And a word that shall echo forevermore!

All: Listen, listen, listen
Listen my children
Regulars are coming, regulars

Reader 1: For, borne on the night-wind of the Past,

Reader 2: through all our history,

Readers 3: to the last

Reader 4: In the hour of darkness and peril and need,

Readers 1-4: The people will waken and listen to hear
The hurrying hoofbeats of that steed,

All: And the midnight message of Paul Revere.

All: Listen, listen, listen
Listen my children
One if by land, two if by sea
Listen, listen, listen
Listen my children and you shall hear
The Regulars are coming, Regulars!
Listen, listen, listen

Shhhhhhhhhhhhhhhhhhhhhhhhhhhhhhhhhhhhhhhhh

NOTE: Although this text is actually written at about a 9th grade reading level, a script breaks it down into smaller pieces to practice. My fourth graders, even at the very beginning of my work on fluency were able to perform it well. In fact, the lowest readers tracked every line by mouthing the words to insure their appropriate entrance. The greatest difficulty was the two speaking parts being done simultaneously. I divided the parts with the boys handling the Readers' parts and the girls whispering loudly the "All" parts. Because this is such a long text involving so many students, I actually acted as a musical director throughout the performance.

Preamble to the Constitution

Script by Lorraine Griffith

A Choral Reading for a large group or a Reader's Theater for 7 voices

R1: The Constitution

R2: of the United States of America.

All: We the people

R1: The people:

R2: First the Native American,

R3: then a flood of Europeans immigrants,

R4: Africans,

R5: Middle Easterners,

R6: Asian peoples,

R7: South Americans

R1-7: and they keep on coming.

All: We the people of the United States,

R1: The United States:

R2: ALL 50!

R3: From Portland, Maine, west to San Diego, California,

R4: from Fargo, North Dakota, south to El Paso, Texas

R5: Alaska and Hawaii

All: We the people of the United States in order to form a more perfect Union,

R6: That Union seemed perfect, all of the colonies became states as well as the territories to the west,

R7: until the southern states seceded because they wanted States Rights.

R1: But the Civil War ended with a more perfect union of states based upon the belief that all Americans deserved the right to life, liberty, and the pursuit of happiness.

All: We the people of the United States, in order to form a more perfect Union, establish justice,

R2: Even before the established United States, justice was valued.

R3: John Adams had actually defended the British in court after they had attacked and killed colonists during the Boston Massacre. Although he didn't believe in the British cause, he still believed justice was more important than retribution.

R4: Justice was ensured for Americans by following the fairness of John Adams in establishing a Court system beginning with local courthouses and moving up to the Supreme Court in Washington, D.C.

Preamble to the Constitution *(cont.)*

All: We the people of the United States, in order to form a more perfect Union, establish justice, insure domestic tranquility,

R5: There have been times when our nation's tranquility has been disturbed.

R6: but in spite of Pearl Harbor, December 7th, 1941,

R7: and as recent as the horror in New York City, Washington, D.C; and Shanksville, Pennsylvania, September 11th, 2001

R1-7: we still live in a stable and peaceful country.

All: We the people of the United States, in order to form a more perfect Union, establish justice, insure domestic tranquility, provide for the common defense,

R2: The Air Force. No one comes close! Soar to new heights in the wild blue yonder!

R3: The Army. Be all you can be! Be an army of one! Hoo Ahh!

R4: The Navy, Welcome aboard; Anchors aweigh!

R1: The Coast Guard, Protecting America, It's our job everyday!

R5: and the Marines. The few, the proud. Semper Fi!

All: We the people of the United States, in order to form a more perfect Union, establish justice, insure domestic tranquility, provide for the common defense, promote the general welfare,

R7: People's basic needs must be met in a country.

R5: Needs for housing, education, transportation, and health care are overseen by our government system.

R6: Labor laws ensure that people work in safe environments and that they are paid fairly for the work that they do.

All: We the people of the United States, in order to form a more perfect Union, establish justice, insure domestic tranquility, provide for the common defense, promote the general welfare, and secure the blessings of liberty to ourselves

R1: Jefferson's promise of Life, Liberty, and the Pursuit of happiness came later for many of the peoples of our nation.

R2: African Americans did not share the rights of whites by law until the Emancipation Proclamation signed in 1863.

R3: Women did not share in the rights of men to vote or own property until 1920 when the Suffrage Act was ratified.

All: We the people of the United States, in order to form a more perfect Union, establish justice, insure domestic tranquility, provide for the common defense, promote the general welfare, and secure the blessings of liberty to ourselves and our posterity,

Preamble to the Constitution *(cont.)*

R1: That's you and me!

R2-3: And our children!

R4-7: And our children's children.

R1-7: And their children too!

All: We the people of the United States, in order to form a more perfect Union, establish justice, insure domestic tranquility, provide for the common defense, promote the general welfare, and secure the blessings of liberty to ourselves and our posterity, do ordain and establish this Constitution for the United States of America.

R5: The Constitution of the United States of America has stood the test of time.

R6: Although it was signed on September 17th, 1787, it still stands as a ruling document of laws, ensuring our rights and liberties that we still enjoy today.

R7: And so, let us proclaim once again for all the world to hear. . . .

R1: The Preamble to the Constitution of the United States of America.

R2-3: We the people of the United States,

R2-3-4-5: in order to form a more perfect Union,

R2-3-4-5-6: establish justice, insure domestic tranquility,

R1-2-3-4-5-6-7: provide for the common defense, promote the general welfare,

ALL: and secure the blessings of liberty, to ourselves and our posterity, do ordain and establish this Constitution for the United States of America.

NOTE: My children love this piece! Taking an historical document and annotating it, is a great way to teach the meaning behind the familiar words. The children were very proud of themselves for memorizing the preamble in the process of learning the script. During a performance for parents on the last part, they all looked up at the audience and recited the preamble from memory. It was very effective.

Adages From Poor Richard's Almanack

By Benjamin Franklin

A Reader's Theater for 6 voices

R1: Tart words make no friends; a spoonful of honey will catch more flies than a gallon of vinegar.

R2: Early to bed, early to rise, makes a man healthy, wealthy, and wise.

R3: Don't throw stones at your neighbors, if your own windows are glass.

R4: A little neglect may breed mischief; for want of a nail the shoe was lost; for want of a shoe the horse was lost; for want of a horse the rider was lost; for want of the rider the battle was lost.

R5: If you know the value of money, go and try to borrow some; he that goes a-borrowing goes a-sorrowing.

R6: If a man could have half his wishes, he would double his troubles.

Two Men Created Equal

Benjamin Banneker and Thomas Jefferson

By Lorraine Griffith

A Reader's Theater for 6 voices

R1-4: Over two hundred years ago, two baby boys were born into very different homes.

R1: One child, the son of a freed slave in Maryland, was educated in a Quaker school and grew up to think creatively in the area of math,

R2: to love inventions, actually carving a wooden clock that kept precise time for forty years,

R1: to study the stars—accurately predicting a solar eclipse in 1789,

R2: to write valuable farmer's almanacs using self-taught calculations,

R1: and to survey a huge plot of land, later becoming the capital of our nation.

R1&2: His name was Benjamin Banneker!

R2: In fact, when the French architect who designed the city of Washington, D.C, stole the plans in a fit of anger, Benjamin Banneker had such an incredible memory, he was able to draft the entire plan for the city from memory.

R3: The other child, was born into a wealthy, white slave-owning family in Virginia.

R4: But like the first child, this boy also grew up to love creatively improving things like the swivel chair and a dumb waiter,

R3: to brilliantly write the Declaration of Independence,

R4: and to design the architecture of his home in Monticello and the University of Virginia.

Two Men Created Equal *(cont.)*

R3&4: His name was Thomas Jefferson!

R3: Later Thomas Jefferson was to become Secretary of State under George Washington, and the third president of the United States of America.

R1-4: There was no reason to think that in the 1790's, these two lives would come together.

R1: Blacks and whites did not run in the same circles during that time before the Civil War,

R2: before Sojourner Truth,

R3: before William Lloyd Garrison,

R4: and before Martin Luther King, Jr.

R1: Prompted by his frustration with the varied social status of blacks and whites in America, Benjamin Banneker considered the writings of the Declaration of Independence.

Jefferson: "We hold these truths to be self-evident, that all men are created equal, that they are endowed by their Creator with certain unalienable Rights, that among these are Life, Liberty and the Pursuit of Happiness. . ."

R2: Banneker decided to boldly write to Thomas Jefferson, the author of those stirring words.

Banneker: "Now, sir, if this is founded in truth, I apprehend you will readily embrace every opportunity to eradicate that train of absurd and false ideas and opinions, which so generally prevails with respect to us (blacks), and that your sentiments are concurrent with mine, which are that one universal Father hath given being to us all, and that He hath not only made us all of one flesh, but that He hath also without partiality afforded us all the same sensations, and endued us all with the same faculties, and that however variable we may be in society or religion, however diversified in situation or color, we are all of the same family, and stand in the same relation to Him."

Two Men Created Equal *(cont.)*

R2: Along with the letter, Banneker sent a copy of his Farmer's Almanac, providing to Jefferson the proof of a brilliant mathematical mind creating such accurate year-long predictions of the movements in the heavens.

R1: Banneker was asking Jefferson to include the black population into the declared truth that "all men are created equal." Jefferson responded with a letter of his own.

Jefferson: I thank you sincerely for your letter of the 19th instant, and of the Almanac it contained. Nobody wishes more than I do to see such proofs as you exhibit, that nature has given our black brethren talents equal to those of other colours of men, and that the appearance of a want of them is owing only to the degraded condition of their existence, both in Africa and America. I can add with truth that no one wishes more ardently to see a good system commenced for raising the condition both of their body and mind to what it ought to be.

R1-4: Although Jefferson's equality never reached Banneker's people in their life times, Banneker's words still resound through to our age . . .

Banneker: However variable we may be in society or religion, however diversified in situation or color, we are all of the same family. . .

NOTE: The most difficult part of this script is the letter from Banneker to Jefferson. You must choose a very fluent reader for this part so that the performance continues at an acceptable pace. The beauty of this requirement though, is that the level of Banneker's vocabulary is embedded textual evidence for his intelligence.

The Mississippi Just Before Dawn

A Sentence from *The Adventures of Huckleberry Finn* by Mark Twain

A Reader's Theater for 4 voices

R1: *The Adventures of Huckleberry Finn* was published in 1884 and is considered Twain's masterpiece and one of the truly great examples of American literature.

R2: The novel is narrated by Huck Finn together with a runaway slave, as Huck makes his way down the Mississippi on a raft. On the aimless journey, Huck and Jim become involved with a series of contrasting characters such as the feuding Grangerford and Shepheredson families and later the suspicious 'Duke' who sells Jim back into slavery. Enormously influential and popular, *Huckleberry Finn*, was also somewhat controversial with its often-racy content and its depictions of the evils of slavery.

R3: The following is one sentence of 284 words, the longest in the book. Some consider it one of the greatest sentences in literature. It describes, in Huck's voice, floating down the Mississippi just before dawn. The sentence. . .

R4: The first thing to see, looking away over the water, was a kind of dull line —that was the woods on the other side—you couldn't make nothing else out;

R1: then a pale place in the sky; then more paleness, spreading around; then the river softened up, away off, and weren't black any more, but gray; you could see little dark spots drifting along, ever so far away

R2: —trading scows,

R3: [large flat bottom boats with square ends, used for transporting freight]

The Mississippi Just Before Dawn *(cont.)*

R2: and such things; and long black streaks—rafts; sometimes you could hear a sweep screaking; or jumbled up voices,

R4: it was so still, and sounds come so far; and by-and-by you could see a streak on the water which you know by the look of the streak that there's a snag there in a swift current which breaks on it and makes that streak look that way;

R1: and you see the mist curl up off of the water, and the east reddens up, and the river,

R2: and you make out a log cabin in the edge of the woods, away on the bank on the other side of the river, being a wood-yard, likely, and piled by them cheats so you can throw a dog through it anywheres;

R3: then the nice breeze springs up, and comes fanning you from over there, so cool and fresh, and sweet to smell, on account of the woods and the flowers;

R4: but sometimes not that way, because they've left dead fish laying around, gars,

R1: [a fish with a long snout, such as a needlefish]

R4: and such, and they do get pretty rank;

R1: and next you've got the full day, and everything smiling in the sun, and the song-birds just going it!

NOTE: The students who perform this script need to study the featured sentence until they are in awe of the scene it describes and can visualize the setting. Reader 4 may want to begin the performance with his or her back to the audience. Then just before he or she begins the sentence, he or she could turn toward the audience as if beginning a new story. I suggest that the students who define words actually create the brackets around their mouths with their hands so that the audience realizes that the definitions are not within the actual text.

O Magnet-South

A poem by Walt Whitman, 1881
Arranged by Kaitlyn Roy & Lorraine Griffith

A Reader's Theater for 4 voices

R1: O magnet-south! O glistening perfumed South!

R2: my South!

R3: O quick mettle,

R4: rich blood,

R3: impulse and love!

R4: good and evil!

R3&4: O all dear to me!

R2: O dear to me my birth-things—all moving things and the trees where I was born—

R1: the grains,

R3: plants,

R4: rivers,

R1: Dear to me my own slow sluggish rivers where they flow, distant, over flats of silver sands or through swamps,

R3: Dear to me the Roanoke,

R4: the Savannah,

R3: the Altamahaw,

R4: the Pedee,

R3: the Tombigbee,

R4: the Santee,

R3: the Coosa

R4: and the Sabine,

R2: O pensive, far away wandering, I return with my soul to haunt their banks again,

R1: Again in Florida I float on transparent lakes, I float on the Okeechobee, I cross the hummock-land or through pleasant openings or dense forests,

R3: I see the parrots in the woods,

R4: I see the papaw-tree and the blossoming titi;

R2: Again, sailing in my coaster on deck, I coast off Georgia, I coast up the Carolinas,

R1: I see where the live-oak is growing, I see where the yellow-pine, the scented bay-tree, the lemon and orange, the cypress, the graceful palmetto,

O Magnet-South *(cont.)*

R3: I pass rude sea-headlands

R4: and enter Pamlico Sound through an inlet,

R3: and dart my vision inland;

R2: O the cotton plant! the growing fields of rice, sugar, hemp!

R1: The cactus guarded with thorns, the laurel-tree with large white flowers,

R3: The range afar,

R4: the richness and barrenness,

R3: the old woods charged with mistletoe

R4: and trailing moss,

R2: The piney odor and the gloom, the awful natural stillness, (here in these dense swamps the freebooter carries his gun, and the fugitive has his conceal'd hut);

R1: O the strange fascination of these half-known half-impassable swamps, infested by reptiles, resounding with the bellow of the alligator, the sad noises of the night-owl and the wild-cat, and the whirr of the rattlesnake,

R3: The mocking-bird,

R4: the American mimic,

R3: singing all the forenoon,

R4: singing through the moon-lit night,

R3: The humming-bird,

R4: the wild turkey,

R3: the raccoon,

R4: the opossum;

R2: A Kentucky corn-field, the tall, graceful, long-leav'd corn, slender, flapping, bright green, with tassels, with beautiful ears each well-sheath'd in its husk; O my heart! O tender and fierce pangs, I can stand them not, I will depart;

R1: O to be a Virginian where I grew up!

R3: O to be a Carolinian!

All: O longings irrepressible!

R4: O I will go back to old Tennessee and never wander more.

NOTE: This script goes well with a unit where the students need to understand the nature of the southeast region of the United States. When discussing the southern role in the Revolutionary War or the War Between the States, it would give information about the topography and foliage of the region. It would also help with the visualization of the setting of a southern novel.

Prelude to the Civil War

Collected by Douglas Vicharelli and Timothy Rasinski

A Reader's Theater for 2 to 18 voices

That all men are by nature equally free and independent and have certain inherent rights.

—*Virginia Declaration of Rights, June 1776*

We hold these truths to be self-evident, that all men are created equal, that they are endowed by their Creator with certain unalienable Rights, that among these are Life, Liberty, and the pursuit of Happiness.

—*Declaration of Independence, July 1776*

The powers not delegated to the United States by the Constitution, nor prohibited by it to the states, are reserved to the states respectively, or to the people.

—*Amendment X, Constitution of the United States*

No more slave States; no slave territories.

—*Senator Salmon P. Chase, Ohio, 1848*

I believe this government cannot endure permanently, half slave and half free.

—*Abraham Lincoln, 1858*

I am now quite certain that the crimes of this guilty land will never be purged away but with blood.

—*John Brown*

Wherever there is a human being, I see God-given rights inherent in that being, whatever the sex or complexion.

—*William Lloyd Garrison*

I pity the poor in bondage that have none to help them; that is why I am here; not to gratify any personal animosity, revenge, or vindictive spirit. It is my sympathy with the oppressed and the wronged, that are as good as you, and as precious in the sight of God.

—*John Brown*

Prelude to the Civil War *(cont.)*

The success of any great moral enterprise does not depend upon numbers.

—*William Lloyd Garrison*

I hear many condemn these men because they were so few. When were the good and the brave ever in a majority? Would you have had him wait till that time came? —till you and I came over to him? The very fact that John Brown had no rabble or troop of hirelings about him would alone distinguish him from ordinary heroes. His company was small indeed, because few could be found worthy to pass muster.

—*Henry David Thoreau*

In firing his gun, John Brown has merely told what time of day it is. It is high noon.

—*William Lloyd Garrison*

I wish to say, furthermore, that you had better, all you people of the South, prepare yourselves for a settlement of that question, that must come up for settlement sooner than you are prepared for it. The sooner you are prepared the better. You may dispose of me very easily. I am nearly disposed of now; but this question is still to be settled— this Negro question, I mean; the end of that is not yet.

—*John Brown*

This will be a great day in our history; the date of a New Revolution —quite as much as needed as the old one. Even now as I write they are leading old John Brown to execution in Virginia for attempting to rescue slaves! This is sowing the wind to reap the whirlwind which will come soon!

—*Henry Wadsworth Longfellow*

Some eighteen hundred years ago Christ was crucified; this morning, perchance, Captain John Brown was hung. These are the two ends of a chain which is not without its links. He is not Old Brown any longer; he is an angel of light.

—*Henry David Thoreau*

John Brown's zeal in the cause of freedom was infinitely superior to mine. Mine was as the taper light; his was as the burning sun. I could live for the slave; John Brown could die for him.

—*Frederick Douglass*

Prelude to the Civil War *(cont.)*

I wish I could say that John Brown was the representative of the North. He was a superior man. He did not value his bodily life in comparison with ideal things. He did not recognize unjust human laws, but resisted them as he was bid. For once we are lifted out of the trivialness and dust of politics into the region of truth and manhood. No man in America has ever stood up so persistently and effectively for the dignity of human nature, knowing himself for a man, and the equal of any and all governments. In that sense he was the most American of us all.

—Henry David Thoreau

There is a terrible war coming, and these young men who have never seen war cannot wait for it to happen, but I tell you, I wish that I owned every slave in the South, for I would free them all to avoid this war.

—Lt. Col. Robert E. Lee, United States Army

Let me tell you what is coming. After the sacrifice of countless millions of treasure and hundreds of thousands of lives you may win Southern independence, but I doubt it. The North is determined to preserve this Union. They are not a fiery, impulsive people as you are, for they live in colder climates. But when they begin to move in a given direction, they move with the steady momentum and perseverance of a mighty avalanche.

—Governor Sam Houston —Texas

What to the American Slave Is Your Fourth of July?

By Frederick Douglass

A Reader's Theater for 4 voices

NARRATOR: You are going to hear a speech given by Frederick Douglass at an Independence Day Celebration in 1852 in Rochester, NY. At that period in history, most black Americans did not observe Independence Day on July 4th. They had not yet found the freedom most white Americans enjoyed. In this speech Douglass fought with words for the freedom of fellow blacks still enslaved. Three speakers will share the powerful words of one articulate man, Frederick Douglass.

ALL: "What to the American slave is your Fourth of July?

R1: Fellow citizens,

R2: pardon me,

R3: allow me to ask,

ALL: Why am I called upon to speak here today?

R3: What have I, or those I represent, to do with your national independence?

R2: Are the great principles of political freedom and of natural justice, embodied in that Declaration of Independence, extended to us?

R1: And am I, therefore, called upon to bring our humble offering to the national altar, and to confess the benefits and express devout gratitude for the blessings resulting from our independence to us?

ALL: What to the American slave is your Fourth of July?

R1: I answer, a day that reveals to him, more than all other days in the year, the gross injustice and cruelty to which he is the constant victim.

What to the American Slave Is Your Fourth of July? *(cont.)*

R2: To him, your celebration is a sham;

R3: your sounds of rejoicing are empty and heartless;

R1: your shouts of liberty and equality hollow mockery;

R2: your prayers and hymns are to him mere fraud and hypocrisy —

R3: a thin veil to cover up crimes which would disgrace a nation of savages.

ALL: There is not a nation on the earth guilty of practices more shocking and bloody, than are the people of these United States, at this very hour.

R1: Go where you may,

R2: search where you will,

R3: roam through all the monarchies and despotisms of the Old World,

R2: travel through South America,

R1: search out every abuse,

R3: and when you have found the last,

ALL: lay your facts by the side of the everyday practices of this nation,

R1: and you will say with me that,

R2: for revolting barbarity and shameless hypocrisy,

R3: America reigns without a rival.

ALL: And I ask again. . . What to the American slave is your Fourth of July?

Frederick Douglass used bold language in this speech. The students who have performed this have struggled with some of the vocabulary like "despotism" and "barbarity." There is a depth to the students' understanding though, of the desperate historical period of which he spoke, by the time they have mastered the script. I chose to divide his words into three speakers' parts because of the difficulty of the vocabulary. If the students increase in intensity throughout the script and keep the flow of his words, the speech in three parts is very effective.

Drum Taps

By Walt Whitman   Arranged by Stephen Griffith

A Reader's Theater for 5 Readers

R1: Walt Whitman was an American poet born in 1819. His collection, "Leaves of Grass" was a continuing work, growing from the original volume of 12 poems published in 1855 to over 300 works at the time of his death in 1892. "Leaves of Grass" is now considered one of the world's major literary works. Although the subject material of "Leaves of Grass" is varied, today we read bits and pieces of the poems he wrote, as an observer, about the War Between the States during the 1860's when over 11% of the population of the United States lost their lives.

ALL READERS: Now hear the words of Walt Whitman.

R2: (pause then loud) BEAT! beat! drums!—Blow! bugles! blow!

Through the windows—through doors—

burst like a ruthless force, into the solemn church,

and scatter the congregation;

Into the school where the scholar is studying;

BEAT! beat! drums!—Blow! bugles! blow!

R3: Beat! beat! drums!—Blow! bugles! blow!

Mind not the timid—

Mind not the weeper or prayer;

Mind not the old man beseeching the young man;

Let not the child's voice be heard, nor the mother's entreaties;

Beat! beat! drums!—Blow! bugles! blow!

ALL READERS: So strong you thump, O terrible drums—

So loud you bugles blow.

R4: To the drum-taps prompt,

The young men falling in and arming.

ALL READERS: BEAT! beat! drums!—Blow! bugles! blow!

R5: The lawyer leaving his office, and arming

—the judge leaving the court;

R4: The driver deserting his wagon in the street, jumping down, throwing the reins abruptly down on the horses' backs;

R5: The salesman leaving the store

—the boss, book-keeper, porter, all leaving;

Drum Taps *(cont.)*

R2:	Squads gather everywhere by common consent, and arm;
ALL READERS:	BEAT! beat! drums!—Blow! bugles! blow!
R4:	Arm'd regiments arrive every day, pass through the city, and embark from the wharves;
R5:	How good they look, as they tramp down to the river, sweaty, with their guns on their shoulders!
R2:	The blood of the city up-arm'd! arm'd! the cry everywhere;
	The flags flung out from the steeples of churches, and from all the public buildings and stores . . .
R4:	The tearful parting-the mother kisses her son—the son kisses his mother . . .
R5:	The unpent enthusiasm—the wild cheers of the crowd . . .
R2:	The artillery—the silent cannons, bright as gold, drawn along, rumble lightly over the stones. . . (Silent cannons-soon to cease your silence! Soon, unlimber'd, to begin the red business);
ALL READERS:	BEAT! beat! drums!—Blow! bugles! blow!
R1:	The swarming ranks press on and on,
	the dense brigades press on;
	Glittering dimly,
	toiling under the sun—
	the dust-cover'd men,
	In columns rise and fall to the undulations of the ground,
	With artillery interspers'd
	—the wheels rumble,
	the horses sweat,
	As the army corps advances.
ALL READERS:	BEAT! beat! drums!—Blow! bugles! blow!
R2:	I see the shells exploding, leaving small white clouds
R3:	I hear the great shells shrieking as they pass;
R4:	The grape, like the hum and whirr of wind through the trees,
R5:	(quick, tumultuous, now the contest rages!)
R1:	All the scenes at the batteries themselves rise in detail before me again;
	The crashing and smoking—the pride of the men in their weapons;

Drum Taps *(cont.)*

ALL READERS: BEAT! beat! drums!—Blow! bugles! blow!

R3: The chief gunner ranges and sights his piece,

and selects a fuse of the right time;

After firing, I see him lean aside, and look eagerly off to note the effect;

R2: Elsewhere I hear the cry of a regiment charging—

(the young colonel leads himself this time, with brandish'd sword);

R1: I breathe the suffocating smoke-

then the flat clouds hover low, concealing all;

Now a strange lull comes for a few seconds,

not a shot fired on either side;

Then resumed, the chaos louder than ever, with eager calls, and orders of officers;

And ever the sound of the cannon

And ever the hastening of infantry shifting positions

Grime, heat, rush

And bombs busting in air

R4: Come up from the fields, father, here's a letter from our Pete;

And come to the front door, mother—here's a letter from thy dear son.

R1: Lo, 'tis autumn;

Lo, where the trees, deeper green, yellower and redder,

Cool and sweeten Ohio's villages, with leaves fluttering in the moderate wind;

Where apples ripe in the orchards hang.

R5: But now from the fields come, father-

Come at the daughter's call;

And come to the entry, mother—

To the front door come, right away.

Fast as she can she hurries—something ominous—

Her steps trembling;

She does not tarry to smoothe her hair, nor adjust her cap.

R4: Open the envelope quickly;

O this is not our son's writing, yet his name is sign'd;

Drum Taps *(cont.)*

R4: O a strange hand writes for our dear son—
O stricken mother's soul!
All swims before her eyes—flashes with black—
She catches the main words only;
Sentences broken—gun-shot wound in the breast, cavalry
skirmish, taken to hospital, at present low, but will soon be better.

R5: Grieve not so, dear mother,
(The just-grown daughter speaks through her sobs;
The little sisters huddle around, speechless and dismay'd);
See, dearest mother, the letter says Pete will soon be better.

R1: Alas, poor boy, he will never be better,
(Nor may-be needs to be better, that brave and simple soul);
While they stand at home at the door,
He is dead already; The only son is dead.

R4: But the mother needs to be better;
She, with thin form, presently drest in black;
By day her meals untouch'd—
Then at night fitfully sleeping, often waking,
In the midnight waking, weeping, longing with one deep longing,
O that she might withdraw unnoticed—
Silent from life, escape and withdraw,
To follow, to seek, to be with her dear dead son.

R2: BEAT! beat! drums!—Blow! bugles! blow!
Through the windows—through doors—
burst like a ruthless force, into the solemn church,
and scatter the congregation;
Into the school where the scholar is studying;
BEAT! beat! drums!—Blow! bugles! blow!

R3: Beat! beat! drums!—Blow! bugles! blow!
Mind not the timid—
mind not the weeper or prayer;
Let not the child's voice be heard, nor the mother's entreaties;
Beat! beat! drums!—Blow! bugles! blow!

ALL READERS: So strong you thump, O terrible drums—
So loud you bugles blow.

NOTE: This Reader's Theater was arranged from 38 pages of Whitman's poetry about the Civil War. My fifth graders had some trouble getting into it, until I sat down with them and we walked through the meaning of the text and the symbolism of the drums and bugles. They did an incredible job performing it.

Gettysburg and Mr. Lincoln's Speech

By Timothy Rasinski

A Reader's Theater for five voices: Narrators 1 and 2; Southern Soldier; Northern Soldier, Abraham Lincoln.

Possible Additional Material: A map, blue and gray caps for the soldiers, stovepipe hat for Mr. Lincoln

Narrator 1: The Civil War was a tragic time in America. It pitted the southern states against the northern states.

Narrator 2: It also pitted brother against brother and friend against friend.

Northern Soldier: I fight to end slavery and to make our country whole again—although we may come from many states, we are one nation and always will be one nation.

Southern Soldier: I fight against the Northerners who try to impose their will on the South, telling us that we have to put an end to slavery, telling us that we cannot live our lives the way that we wish.

Narrator 1: The war was a bloody one. More soldiers died in the Civil War than in any other war that the United States has ever taken part in.

Narrator 2: Through the first few years of the Civil War, the southern or Confederate army, under General Robert E. Lee, won battle after battle against the North.

Southern Soldier: One of us rebels can whip the tar out of ten Yankees!

Northern Soldier: We are good soldiers and we're ready to fight. Our generals, however, are no match for the confederate generals—Robert E. Lee and Stonewall Jackson.

Narrator 1: By 1863 General Lee felt strong enough to invade Pennsylvania, an important northern state. By taking the war to the north, Lee thought that he could convince the North to give up its attempt to reunite the states and end slavery.

Gettysburg and
Mr. Lincoln's Speech *(cont.)*

Narrator 2: The Union Army under General George Meade knew that it had to stop the Confederates. It met up with the southern army during the first three days of July, 1863, in a small Pennsylvania town called. . . .

All: GETTYSBURG!

Narrator 1: For three days, under the hot summer sun the two huge armies struggled.

Southern Soldier: Long live the Confederacy!

Northern Soldier: Union forever! Rally round the flag boys!

Narrator 2: The battle swung back and forth over those blistering hot days. It finally ended in a failed attempt by the confederates to break through the line of Northern soldiers.

Southern Soldier: We called it Pickett's Charge. It was a disaster. Thousands of gray clad soldiers were cut down in the murderous fire coming from the Yankee lines.

Narrator 1: Pickett's Charge failed and Lee knew he had lost the battle. He knew he had to withdraw his army to Virginia, his home state. . . , friendlier territory.

Narrator 2: And so Lee moved his battered and defeated army from Pennsylvania on the evening of July third. He had to leave so quickly that many of the dead and wounded southern soldiers were left lying on the battlefield.

Southern Soldier: We didn't want to leave our fallen brothers lying on Northern soil. But we had to retreat south or risk being annihilated by the victorious Yankees.

Narrator 1: Meade's Army of the Potomac followed Lee out of Pennsylvania, hoping to catch up with him and complete the destruction of the southern army. He too left many of his dead lying on the Gettysburg Battlefield. All told, nearly forty-thousand soldiers, northern and southern were killed, wounded, or missing at Gettysburg.

Gettysburg and Mr. Lincoln's Speech *(cont.)*

Northern Soldier: We tasted sweet victory at last. Now we wanted to finally put an end to this bloody war. We had to chase the enemy wherever he may go.

Narrator 2: But for the people living in Gettysburg, the battle was far from over. When the few thousand residents of Gettysburg returned to their homes, they were greeted by the sight of death.

Narrator 1: Something had to be done quickly to prevent the spread of disease from all the dead and decaying bodies.

Narrator 2: In previous battles, bodies of dead soldiers were sent to their hometowns for burial.

Narrator 1: But this was not possible at Gettysburg. There were simply too many dead and not enough workers to prepare the bodies for transport home. It would take too long.

Narrator 2: The governor of Pennsylvania then made an important decision: the dead soldiers would be buried in a new cemetery in Gettysburg. Burying the bodies in Gettysburg could be accomplished quickly. The threat from the spread of disease could be averted. All the northern states were asked to contribute money for the cemetery for the Gettysburg dead.

Northern Soldier: And so, from July to November, in that year 1863, workers gathered the bodies of our fallen comrades and buried them in the new cemetery.

Southern Soldier: Even some of our southern martyrs were buried at Gettysburg.

Narrator 1: By November, the cemetery was finished. By November, the country understood just how important the battle of Gettysburg was. No more would the confederate army threaten the northern states. The confederacy had reached its high mark and was now in decline.

Gettysburg and Mr. Lincoln's Speech *(cont.)*

Narrator 2: Thus it was decided that a dedication for the cemetery should take place to honor those northern soldiers who made the ultimate sacrifice at Gettysburg.

Narrator 1: Dignitaries from around the country were invited. President Lincoln came. The greatest orator, or speech maker, of the day, Edward Everett, was also asked to give a grand speech. He spoke for over two hours.

Narrator 2: Those who came to the dedication were tired and wanted to go home by the time that Everett had finished his long speech.

Narrator 1: But then President Lincoln was asked to make a few brief remarks.

Narrator 2: Slowly, and so very deliberately, President Lincoln stood up and made his way to the podium. Quietly, he faced the crowd of public dignitaries and ordinary citizens standing in front of him. Somberly, he looked over the countless rows of dead soldiers behind him. And, in just 272 words, Mr. Lincoln helped all of us, those living in 1863 and those of us alive today, understand what is special about our country and why it could not be broken up into free and slave, Union and Confederate, north and south.

Lincoln: Four score and seven years ago, our fathers brought forth on this continent, a new nation, conceived in liberty, and dedicated to the proposition that all men are created equal.

Narrator 1: Lincoln uses words from the Declaration of Independence to remind us why the United States was founded in the first place.

Lincoln: Now we are engaged in a great civil war, testing whether that nation, or any nation so conceived and so dedicated, can long endure.

We are met on a great battlefield of that war.

We have come to dedicate a portion of that field, as a final resting place for those who here gave their lives that the nation might live. It is altogether fitting and proper that we should do this.

Gettysburg and Mr. Lincoln's Speech *(cont.)*

Lincoln: But in a larger sense, we cannot dedicate, we cannot consecrate, we cannot hallow this ground.

The brave men, living and dead, who struggled here, have consecrated it, far beyond our poor power to add or detract.

Narrator 2: Although the dedication that Lincoln was speaking at was meant to make this land special, Lincoln knew, and he told the audience, that the brave soldiers who fought here that summer had made it much more special through their actions than by anything Lincoln could say or do.

Lincoln: The world will little note nor long remember what we say here. But it can never forget what they did here. It is for us the living, rather, to be dedicated here to the unfinished work which they who fought here have thus far so nobly advanced.

It is rather for us to be here dedicated to the great task remaining before us.

That from these honored dead we take increased devotion to that cause for which they gave the last full measure of devotion.

Narrator 1: Although the soldiers who died here saved the Union, much fighting, and much hard work still needs to be done before the nation is made whole again.

Narrator 2: Lincoln realized that the United States was a grand and never-tried-before experiment for all the world to see—can a government created by its citizens and run by its citizens truly work? The world was watching and waiting to find out.

Lincoln: That we here highly resolve that these dead shall not have died in vain. That this nation, under God, shall have a new birth of freedom.

And that. . . . . Government of the people, by the people, for the people, shall not perish from the earth.

Sojourner Truth and the Struggle for People's Equality

By Timothy Rasinski

A Reader's Theater for 5 voices: Narrators 1 through 4 (can be combined), Sojourner Truth

Narrator 1: Long before the civil rights movement of the 1950s and 60s in which certain Americans demanded that all citizens, regardless of the color of their skin, be treated fairly and with respect—

Narrator 2: Indeed, long before the women's rights movement of the 1960s and 70s in which women demanded their right to be treated justly and with dignity—

Narrator 3: Even years before the start of the Civil War, a war fought to end slavery in the United States—

Narrator 4: There were people who spoke up for the rights of black people and the rights of women. One of those people was

Narrators 1, 2, 3, 4: Sojourner Truth.

Narrator 1: Sojourner Truth was a black woman, a Negro, and she was born into slavery in 1797.

Narrator 2: But she was not afraid to speak out for what she thought was right and against what she knew was wrong.

Narrator 3: In the years before the Civil War, she spoke throughout the northern and midwestern United States, to whomever would listen to her, about the evils of slavery and the need for all Americans to have equal rights.

Narrator 4: She was a powerful speaker. And since she stood six feet tall, people listened to what she had to say!

Narrator 1: In the 1850s, women in the United States did not have the same rights as men. They could not vote, they could not go to college, they could not own their own property.

Narrator 2: In many ways they were the property of their husbands— almost like slaves themselves. Men did not think women were strong enough or smart enough to have the same rights as men.

Sojourner Truth and the Struggle for People's Equality *(cont.)*

Narrator 3: Many men thought that women were weak, that they needed to be helped into carriages, that they needed to be carried over ditches, that they needed to be taken care of by men.

Narrator 4: Besides, since Jesus Christ was a man, many men felt that that must be proof that men were superior to women and that women did not deserve the same rights as men.

Narrator 1: Women knew that this was not right and they began to speak out about this blatant unfairness.

Narrator 2: They began to organize meetings in which they spoke out about their lack of rights.

Narrator 3: But these meetings were run by white women, mostly from the northern states. Black women were neither welcome nor wanted.

Narrator 4: In 1851, a women's rights convention was held in Akron, Ohio. And many women and men spoke about the rights of women— white women that is.

Narrator 1: But in the middle of the convention, a tall black woman stood up and demanded to speak. Those at the meeting tried to keep her from speaking. They protested her presence loudly and they demanded that she leave.

Narrator 2: This is a meeting for whites only, get her out of here.

Narrator 3: No Blacks allowed here.

Narrator 4: Let her speak to her own people. Make her leave.

Narrator 1: But Sojourner Truth was not only tall, she was strong in her beliefs. And she made her way to the podium, faced the group of angry white people, waited a few seconds— and told everyone that the struggle for rights of white women was the struggle for all women, regardless of the color of their skin.

Sojourner Truth and the Struggle for People's Equality *(cont.)*

Sojourner: Well, children, where there is so much racket there must be something out of kilter. I think that between the Negroes of the South and the women of the North, all talking about rights, the white men will be in a fix pretty soon. But what's all this here talking about? That man over there says that women need to be helped into carriages, and lifted over ditches, and to have the best of everything. Nobody ever helps me into carriages, or over mud-puddles, or gives me the best of anything! And ain't I a woman? Look at me! Look at my arm. I have plowed and planted, and gathered into barns, and no man could head me! And ain't I a woman? I could work as much and eat as much as man — when I could get it — and I could bear the lash as well! And ain't I a woman? I have borne thirteen children, and have seen most all of them sold off to slavery, and when I cried out with my mother's grief, none but Jesus heard me! And ain't I a woman?

Narrator 2: By now the crowd was hushed. Sojourner's strong voice presided over the crowd. A silence descended on the audience. Heads began to nod in response to Sojourner's repeated question—Ain't I a woman?

Sojourner: Then they talk about this thing in the head; what's this they call it?

Narrator 3: You mean intellect?

Sojourner: That's it honey. What's that got to do with women's rights or Negroes' rights? If my cup won't hold but a pint, and your holds a quart, wouldn't you be mean not to let me have my little half-measure?

Then that little man in black over there, he says that women can't have as much rights as men, cause Christ wasn't a woman! Where did your Christ come from? Where did your Christ come from? From God and a woman! Man had nothing to do with it.

Sojourner Truth and the Struggle for People's Equality *(cont.)*

Sojourner: If the first woman God ever made was strong enough to turn the world upside down all alone, these women together ought to be able to turn it back, and get it right side up again! And now that they is asking to do it, the men better let them.

Obliged to you for hearing me, and now old Sojourner ain't got nothing more to say.

(Silence for a few seconds)

Narrator 4: And with that, her speech was over. Sojourner Truth left the podium and she walked out of the meeting and into history. Yet her words still ring true today as they did on that day in 1851—

Narrator 1: Ain't I a Woman?

Narrator 2: Even though the color of my skin may be different from yours, inside we are all the same.

Narrator 3: And I too deserve to be treated with equality, respect, and dignity.

Franklin Roosevelt and the Great Depression

By Timothy Rasinski

A Reader's Theater for 6 voices: Narrators 1 and 2, Citizens 1 and 2, President Hoover, President Roosevelt
(Optional: Fade from song "Brother Can you Spare a Dime.")

Narrator 1: Thursday October 24, 1929, was a terrible day in American history and it has come to be called Black Thursday—on that day the bottom dropped out of the stock market. Over the next several days people lost over half the value of their investments in the stock market. Fortunes were lost and the economy began a slide into the worst ten year slump the United States has ever known.

N2: That economic slump that began with the crash of the Stock Market is better known as the Great Depression.

N1: During the Great Depression people not only lost all of their money as banks closed down. People also lost their jobs, families lost their homes, many adults and children went hungry. Others had to beg for food and clothing.

N2: At about this same time, severe droughts and dust storms hit parts of the Midwest and Southwest United States. Thousands of farm families were wiped out.

N1: Some people became so distressed by their lost fortunes, they committed suicide.

N2: The president at the beginning of the Great Depression was Herbert Hoover. Hoover vetoed several bills aimed at using the federal government to relieve people's economic distress brought on by the depression because he felt that such actions would give the federal government in Washington too much power.

Hoover: Government should not intrude too deeply into the lives of people. I believe that American business, if left alone to operate without government supervision, will eventually correct the economic conditions now plaguing the country and return the United States to prosperity. Better times are just around the corner. We must have patience.

Franklin Roosevelt and the Great Depression *(cont.)*

N1: But prosperity was not just around the next corner. The Great Depression continued and deepened. Many people who lost their homes were forced to live in shacks made from the crates and flattened tin cans in the shabbiest parts of town. These growing cities of shacks and rubble came to be known as Hoovervilles—

N2: A name that reflected the people's anger and disappointment at President Hoover's failure to act to relieve people's misery and attempt to end the depression.

N1: People suffered terribly during the Great Depression.

Citizen 1: I owned a farm in Nebraska. When the prices for wheat and corn were good I bought more land to expand my farm. I used loans from the bank to finance my land purchases. But when the Depression hit, the price for the wheat and corn that I grew fell and fell. I couldn't make a profit from the food that I grew. I couldn't repay my loans. . . and I lost my entire farm—the bank took it away. . . the farm that my grandparents had homesteaded 50 years ago.

Citizen 2: I worked in Detroit at the Ford Motor Company—I helped Henry Ford build the cars that put America on wheels in the 1920s. But then came the Depression. America wasn't much interested in buying cars. And so I lost my job. Without a steady income, I couldn't afford to make my house payments. And so I lost my house. My family was forced to move in with my own parents. Instead of working in a factory, making a good wage, I now sold apples and pencils from a street corner downtown. How can a person make a living selling apples and pencils?

Citizen 1: I was a farmer in Oklahoma. When we entered a prolonged drought, our land turned to dust and blew away. It was called the dust bowl—the land was not fit for people or animals. Many of us picked up what belongings we could put into our cars and trucks and moved to California where we thought life might be a bit easier.

Franklin Roosevelt and the Great Depression *(cont.)*

Citizen 2: I am an army veteran of World War I—the War to End all Wars it was called. When I went to Washington, D.C, with my fellow veterans, (we were known as the Bonus Army) to ask for the bonus money that had been promised to us veterans by Congress, President Hoover sent the regular army under General Douglas MacArthur to chase us out of town. Needless to say I do not have a very favorable impression of Mr. Hoover.

Citizen 1: I owned stocks and I had money saved in the banks. But when the stock market crashed and the banks closed down, I lost all of my money. I couldn't afford to take care of my family. I thought about committing suicide so that my wife could collect money on my life insurance policy. Many of my business friends had taken their lives in this way. Should I?

Citizen 2: The hit song of the day was entitled "Brother, Can You Spare a Dime." And you know, most people did not have enough money to give ten lousy cents to someone who was hungry and out of work.

N1: Finally, with the next presidential election in 1932, the country had had enough of President Hoover and his do nothing attitude. He was defeated by the democratic candidate Franklin Roosevelt. Roosevelt promised to put government to work to help people make it through this long and severe economic depression.

Citizen 1: Now we sang a new song—It was called "Happy Days are Here Again"—at least we thought with Mr. Roosevelt as President, happy days might just be right around the corner.

N2: At his inauguration in 1933, President Roosevelt made a famous speech in which he laid out his plans for how government would help the people. His first point was to calm the fears that so many Americans had for their futures and the future of their country.

Roosevelt: This is preeminently the time to speak the truth, the whole truth, frankly and boldly. So, first of all, let me assert my firm belief that—the only thing we have to fear is fear itself—nameless, unreasoning, unjustified terror which paralyzes needed efforts to convert retreat into advance.

Franklin Roosevelt and the Great Depression *(cont.)*

N1: But Roosevelt recognized that mere words, encouraging words, hopeful words were not enough to move the country back to prosperity.

Roosevelt: This nation asks for action, and action now! Our greatest primary task is to put people to work. This is no unsolvable problem if we face it wisely and courageously. It can be accomplished in part by direct recruiting by the government itself, treating the task as we would treat the emergency of a war, but at the same time accomplishing greatly needed projects to stimulate and reorganize the use of our natural resources.

N2: Roosevelt's words foreshadowed what he would do in the coming months—put Americans to work through government programs that built schools, constructed roads and bridges, provided electric power to rural areas, preserved forests, and developed public parks. These programs would come to be called the Civilian Conservation Corp or CCC, the Works Progress Administration or WPA, and the Tennessee Valley Authority or TVA.

N1: All of these programs, and others, were part of the larger Roosevelt program called the New Deal. A new chance at prosperity for America and all Americans, the New Deal changed the way government worked, it helped relieve the misery of the depression, and it renewed the confidence of Americans in themselves and their government.

N2: Roosevelt's work was appreciated by most Americans. Because of his courage to face the Great Depression and help the American people, he was reelected president for three more terms. He served as president longer than any other president in American history.

Roosevelt: We do not distrust the future of our essential democracy. The people of the United State have not failed. In their need they have registered a mandate, an order, that they want direct and vigorous action. They have asked for discipline and direction under leadership. They have made me the present instrument of their wishes. In the spirit of the gift I take it. In this dedication of a nation we humbly ask the blessing of God. May He protect each and every one of us. May He guide me in the days to come.

(Optional: Fade to song "Happy Days are Here Again.")

The Promise of America

By Mrs. Griffith's 4th Grade Class (2000-2001), based on a quote by Thomas Wolfe

A Reader's Theater for a whole class

All: So then to every man his chance. To every man regardless of his birth his shining golden opportunity. To every man, the right to live, to work, to be himself and to become whatever thing his manhood and his vision can combine to make him. This, seeker, is the promise of America

All: So then to every man his chance—

R1: Excuse me! I'm Molly Pitcher and I had a chance even though I was a woman! In the Revolutionary War I first served soldiers water from my pitcher. But after my husband fainted from the heat, I saw my chance and shot a cannon.

R2: And I had a chance! I'm Martin Luther King, Jr. I spoke for black people! I spoke the truth. I am happy every time I see my children play, talk and attend the same schools together. I had a chance. I used it wisely.

R3: I'm Andrew Jackson! Even though I grew up poor just south of Waxhaw, North Carolina, I worked my way to the top. I defeated the Redcoats because of my thinking. I became the 7th president. I took hold of my chance.

R4: I got a chance to fight for the Americans in the American Revolution. George Washington gave me a high rank and I fought like a wildcat. But I wanted more money and higher ranks so I turned to the British side. You've probably heard of me! I'm Benedict Arnold and I blew my chance to be an American hero!

All: To every man regardless of his birth

R5: I was born a slave. I'm Crispus Attucks. I was a runaway slave and grabbed a chance to fight for freedom. I died in the Boston Massacre! I was the first African American to die in the Revolutionary War.

R6: I was born a slave. I'm a black woman named Sojourner Truth. I spoke up for women's rights and not just black women's rights. I spoke for the rights of everyone. I believed all women, black and white, should have an equal amount of rights compared to men.

The Promise of America *(cont.)*

R7: I was born a woman. I'm Deborah Sampson, but I wanted to fight in the American Revolution. I dressed as a man and joined the army. They only time they found out I was a woman was when I got sick and had to see a doctor.

R8: I was born a black woman. I'm Rosa Parks. I belicved I should have the right to sit in the front seat of the bus like white people. People should sit where they like on the bus. . . . regardless of their birth.

All: His shining golden opportunity—

R9: I, Benjamin Banneker, was given an opportunity to be a farmer, mathematician, and surveyor. I had a golden opportunity to change the attitude toward black people when I was invited to help plan the city of Washington, D.C.

R10: As a black woman in the 1700's, I, Phillis Wheatley, was the first black American poet. George Washington read my poems and published them. I made use of my golden opportunity to write poems.

All: To every man the right to live—

R11: I am the person who signed his name, John Hancock, in huge letters on the Declaration of Independence! I risked my life for my country. If we had lost the revolution, I would have been one of the first ones killed by the British for treason.

R12: I am Benjamin Franklin. Even though I invented great things and could have had a career in science, I chose to risk my life twice—I am the only person who signed both the Declaration of Independence and the Constitution. I tried my best to live for my country.

R13: As Ethan Allen, I wasn't one of the most well-known leaders of the Revolution. But I led the Green Mountain boys at Fort Ticonderoga and fought for Americans to have the right to live the way they wanted!

All: To work.—

The Promise of America *(cont.)*

R14: I, Washington Irving, was blessed as a young boy by George Washington, my namesake. I am the first American author of short stories in the United States. I was able to live in a country where I could write what I liked and work as much as I wanted.

R15: I, Thomas Wolfe, grew up in Asheville, North Carolina! I was given the right to work, the right to be a poet, the right to write about something that I believed in. I took advantage of having the right to write!

All: To be himself and to become whatever thing his manhood and his vision can combine to make him.—

R16: I, John Paul Jones, wanted to be a sailor even though my family hated the idea! I had the right to be myself and to fight for Americans as a sailor. I am famous for saying, "I have not yet begun to fight."

R17: I, Patrick Henry, wanted to be free from the rule of England. So I wrote speeches about being free. Writing speeches was like my hobby! It was being myself. I am famous for saying, "Give me liberty or give me death!"

R18: I, George Washington, was happy to be a farmer and surveyor. But as I grew into leadership in Virginia, I communicated a vision for our young country. After I led our Continental Army to victory over the British, many Americans wanted me to be the new king. But I believed in democracy and became the first president of the United States.

All: This, seeker, is the promise of America.

This Reader's Theater happened in about an hour! We had said the Thomas Wolfe quotation daily during the school year. At the close of an American Revolution unit, I posted the quote divided into individual phrases on the white board. During the unit, each student had done a reading/writing project based on a biography. I asked each student to write their assigned hero on an index card and place it under the phrase they thought most applied to their hero. The kids then wrote a few sentences in first person, and handed them in to me. I put them in order, and voila! We had a Reader's Theater to rehearse and present to parents at the end of the school year!

Casey at the Bat

By "Phin," 1888

A Reader's Theater for 4 voices

Note: The mood changes often and quickly in this script. Be sure you are focusing on the mood of your line and that your voice reflects the mood.

R1: The outlook wasn't brilliant for the Mudville nine that day;

R2: The score stood four to two with but one inning more to play.

R3: And then when Cooney died at first,

R4: and Barrows did the same,

R1: A sickly silence fell upon the patrons of the game.

R1 & 2: A straggling few got up to go in deep despair.

R3 & 4: The rest clung to that hope which springs eternal in the human breast;

They thought if only Casey could but get a whack at that–

R1 & 2: We'd put up even money now with Casey at the bat.

R1: But Flynn preceded Casey,

R2: as did also Jimmy Blake,

R1: And the former was a lulu

R2: and the latter was a cake;

R1 & 2: So upon that stricken multitude grim melancholy sat,

For there seemed but little chance of Casey's getting to the bat.

R3: But Flynn let drive a single, to the wonderment of all,

R4: And Blake, the much despised, tore the cover off the ball;

R3 & 4: And when the dust had lifted, and the men saw what had occurred,

There was Johnnie safe at second and Flynn a-hugging third.

R3: Then from 5,000 throats and more there rose a lusty yell;

R4: It rumbled through the valley,

R1: it rattled in the dell;

R2: It knocked upon the mountain and recoiled upon the flat,

Casey at the Bat *(cont.)*

ALL: For Casey, mighty Casey, was advancing to the bat.

R1: There was ease in Casey's manner as he stepped into his place;

R2: There was pride in Casey's bearing

R3: and a smile on Casey's face.

R4: And when, responding to the cheers, he lightly doffed his hat,

ALL: No stranger in the crowd could doubt 'twas Casey at the bat.

ALL: Ten thousand eyes were on him as he rubbed his hands with dirt;

Five thousand tongues applauded when he wiped them on his shirt.

R1: Then while the writhing pitcher ground the ball into his hip,

R2 & 3: Defiance gleamed in Casey's eye, a sneer curled Casey's lip.

R4: And now the leather-covered sphere came hurtling through the air,

R3: And Casey stood a-watching it in haughty grandeur there.

R1: Close by the sturdy batsman the ball unheeded sped –

R2: "That ain't my style,"

R1: said Casey.

R3: "Stri-i-i-i-i-i-ike one,"

R4: the umpire said.

R2: From the benches black with people,

R3: there went up a muffled roar,

Like the beating of the storm-waves on a stern and distant shore.

R1: "Kill him! Kill the umpire!"

R4: shouted someone on the stand;

R2: And it's likely they'd have killed him had not Casey raised his hand.

Casey at the Bat *(cont.)*

R1: With a smile of Christian charity great Casey's visage shone;

R2: He stilled the rising tumult;

R4: he bade the game go on;

R2: He signaled to the pitcher, and once more the spheroid flew;

R1: But Casey still ignored it,

R4: and the umpire said,

R3: " Stri-i-i-i-i-i-ike two."

R1, 2, 4: "Fraud!"

R3: cried the maddened thousands,

R1: and echo answered

R2, 4: fraud;

R1: But one scornful look from Casey and the audience was awed.

R2: They saw his face grow stern and cold,

R3: they saw his muscles strain,

R4: And they knew that Casey wouldn't let that ball go by again.

R1: The sneer is gone from Casey's lip,

R2: his teeth are clenched in hate;

R3: He pounds with cruel violence his bat upon the plate.

R4: And now the pitcher holds the ball,

R1: and now he lets it go,

R2 & 3: And now the air is shattered by the force of Casey's blow.

R1: Oh, somewhere in this favored land the sun is shining bright;

R2: The band is playing somewhere,

R3: and somewhere hearts are light,

R4: And somewhere men are laughing,

R1: and somewhere children shout;

R2: But there is no joy in Mudville -

R4: mighty Casey has

R3: stru-u-u-u-u-u-uck out!

Note: There are a number of versions of Reader's Theater scripts based on this poem. I chose to shorten the parts so that the participation of the students reflects the participation of the community in a mutual hope that Casey would save the day. The students must see the rise and fall of the action in this text in order to interpret it effectively.

Who's on First?

By Abbott and Costello

A Radio Play for two voices

Abbott: Well, Costello, I'm going to New York with you. You know Bookie Harris, the Yankee's manager, gave me a job as coach for as long as you're on the team.

Costello: Look Abbott, if you're the coach, you must know all the players.

Abbott: I certainly do.

Costello: Well you know I've never met the guys. So you'll have to tell me their names, and then I'll know who's playing on the team.

Abbott: Oh, I'll tell you their names, but you know it seems to me they give these ball players now-a-days very peculiar names.

Costello: You mean funny names?

Abbott: Strange names, pet names. . . like Dizzy Dean. . .

Costello: His brother Daffy.

Abbott: Daffy Dean . . .

Costello: And their French cousin.

Abbott: French?

Costello: Goofè.

Abbott: Goofè Dean. Well, let's see, we have on the bags, Who's on first, What's on second, I Don't Know is on third. . .

Costello: That's what I want to find out.

Abbott: I say Who's on first, What's on second, I Don't Know's on third.

Costello: Are you the manager?

Abbott: Yes.

Costello: You gonna be the coach too?

Abbott: Yes.

Costello: And you don't know the fellows' names?

Abbott: Well I should.

Costello: Well then who's on first?

Abbott: Yes.

Who's on First? *(cont.)*

Costello: I mean the fellow's name.

Abbott: Who.

Costello: The guy on first.

Abbott: Who.

Costello: The first baseman.

Abbott: Who.

Costello: The guy playing. . .

Abbott: Who is on first!

Costello: I'm asking YOU who's on first.

Abbott: That's the man's name.

Costello: That's who's name?

Abbott: Yes.

Costello: Well go ahead and tell me.

Abbott: That's it.

Costello: That's who?

Abbott: Yes.

PAUSE

Costello: Look, you gotta first baseman?

Abbott: Certainly.

Costello: Who's playing first?

Abbott: That's right.

Costello: When you pay off the first baseman every month, who gets the money?

Abbott: Every dollar of it.

Costello: All I'm trying to find out is the fellow's name on first base.

Abbott: Who.

Costello: The guy that gets. . .

Abbott: That's it.

Costello: Who gets the money. . .

Abbott: He does, every dollar. Sometimes his wife comes down and collects it.

Who's on First? *(cont.)*

Costello: Who's wife?

Abbott: Yes.

PAUSE

Abbott: What's wrong with that?

Costello: Look, all I wanna know is when you sign up the first baseman, how does he sign his name?

Abbott: Who.

Costello: The guy.

Abbott: Who.

Costello: How does he sign. . .

Abbott: That's how he signs it.

Costello: Who?

Abbott: Yes.

PAUSE

Costello: All I'm trying to find out is what's the guy's name on first base.

Abbott: No. What is on second base.

Costello: I'm not asking you who's on second.

Abbott: Who's on first.

Costello: One base at a time!

Abbott: Well, don't change the players around.

Costello: I'm not changing nobody!

Abbott: Take it easy, buddy.

Costello: I'm only asking you, who's the guy on first base?

Abbott: That's right.

Costello: Ok.

Abbott: All right.

PAUSE

Costello: What's the guy's name on first base?

Abbott: No. What is on second.

Costello: I'm not asking you who's on second.

Abbott: Who's on first.

Who's on First? *(cont.)*

Costello: I don't know.

Abbott: He's on third, we're not talking about him.

Costello: Now how did I get on third base?

Abbott: Why you mentioned his name.

Costello: If I mentioned the third baseman's name, who did I say is playing third?

Abbott: No. Who's playing first.

Costello: What's on base?

Abbott: What's on second.

Costello: I don't know.

Abbott: He's on third.

Costello: There I go, back on third again!

PAUSE

Costello: Would you just stay on third base and don't go off it.

Abbott: All right, what do you want to know?

Costello: Now who's playing third base?

Abbott: Why do you insist on putting Who on third base?

Costello: What am I putting on third.

Abbott: No. What is on second.

Costello: You don't want Who on second?

Abbott: Who is on first.

Costello: I don't know.

Abbott & Costello Together: Third base!

PAUSE

Costello: Look, you gotta outfield?

Abbott: Sure.

Costello: The left fielder's name?

Abbott: Why.

Costello: I just thought I'd ask you.

Abbott: Well, I just thought I'd tell ya.

Who's on First? *(cont.)*

Costello: Then tell me who's playing left field.

Abbott: Who's playing first.

Costello: I'm not. . . stay out of the infield! I want to know what's the guy's name in left field?

Abbott: No, What is on second.

Costello: I'm not asking you who's on second.

Abbott: Who's on first!

Costello: I don't know.

Abbott & Costello Together: Third base!

PAUSE

Costello: The left fielder's name?

Abbott: Why.

Costello: Because!

Abbott: Oh, he's centerfield.

PAUSE

Costello: Look, You gotta pitcher on this team?

Abbott: Sure.

Costello: The pitcher's name?

Abbott: Tomorrow.

Costello: You don't want to tell me today?

Abbott: I'm telling you now.

Costello: Then go ahead.

Abbott: Tomorrow!

Costello: What time?

Abbott: What time what?

Costello: What time tomorrow are you gonna tell me who's pitching?

Abbott: Now listen. Who is not pitching.

Costello: I'll break your arm, you say who's on first! I want to know what's the pitcher's name?

Who's on First? *(cont.)*

Abbott:	What's on second.
Costello:	I don't know.
Abbott & Costello Together:	Third base!

PAUSE

Costello:	Gotta a catcher?
Abbott:	Certainly.
Costello:	The catcher's name?
Abbott:	Today.
Costello:	Today, and tomorrow's pitching.
Abbott:	Now you've got it.
Costello:	All we got is a couple of days on the team.

PAUSE

Costello:	You know I'm a catcher too.
Abbott:	So they tell me.
Costello:	I get behind the plate to do some fancy catching, Tomorrow's pitching on my team and a heavy hitter gets up. Now the heavy hitter bunts the ball. When he bunts the ball, me, being a good catcher, I'm gonna throw the guy out at first base. So I pick up the ball and throw it to who?
Abbott:	Now that's the first thing you've said right.
Costello:	I don't even know what I'm talking about!

PAUSE

Abbott:	That's all you have to do.
Costello:	Is to throw the ball to first base.
Abbott:	Yes!
Costello:	Now who's got it?
Abbott:	Naturally.

PAUSE

Costello:	Look, if I throw the ball to first base, somebody's gotta get it. Now who has it?

Who's on First? *(cont.)*

Abbott: Naturally.

Costello: Who?

Abbott: Naturally.

Costello: Naturally?

Abbott: Naturally.

Costello: So I pick up the ball and I throw it to Naturally.

Abbott: No you don't, you throw the ball to Who.

Costello: Naturally.

Abbott: That's different.

Costello: That's what I said.

Abbott: You're not saying it. . .

Costello: I throw the ball to Naturally.

Abbott: You throw it to Who.

Costello: Naturally.

Abbott: That's it.

Costello: That's what I said!

Abbott: You ask me.

Costello: I throw the ball to who?

Abbott: Naturally.

Costello: Now you ask me.

Abbott: You throw the ball to Who?

Costello: Naturally.

Abbott: That's it.

Costello: Same as you! Same as YOU! I throw the ball to who. Whoever it is drops the ball and the guy runs to second. Who picks up the ball and throws it to What. What throws it to I Don't Know. I Don't Know throws it back to Tomorrow, Triple play. Another guy gets up and hits a long fly ball to Because. Why? I don't know! He's on third and I don't give a darn!

Abbott: What?

Costello: I said I don't give a darn!

Abbott: Oh, that's our shortstop.

When the Frost Is on the Punkin

By James Whitcomb Riley, 1853-1916

Arranged by Lorraine Griffith

A Reader's Theater for 6 voices

R1: When the frost is on the punkin

R2: and the fodder's in the shock,

R3: And you hear the kyouck and gobble of the struttin' turkey-cock,

R4: And the clackin' of the guineys,

R5: and the cluckin' of the hens,

R6: And the rooster's hallylooer as he tiptoes on the fence;

R1: O, it's then the time a feller is a-feelin' at his best, with the risin' sun to greet him from a night of peaceful rest, as he leaves the house, bareheaded, and goes out to feed the stock,

ALL: When the frost is on the punkin and the fodder's in the shock.

R2: They's something kindo' harty-like about the atmusfere when the heat of summer's over and the coolin' fall is here—

R3: Of course we miss the flowers, and the blossoms on the trees, and the mumble of the hummin'-birds and buzzin' of the bees;

R4: But the air's so appetizin'; and the landscape through the haze of a crisp and sunny morning of the airly autumn days is a pictur' that no painter has the colorin' to mock—

ALL: When the frost is on the punkin and the fodder's in the shock.

R5: The husky,

R6: rusty russel

R1: of the tossels of the corn,

R2: And the raspin' of the tangled leaves as golden as the morn;

R3: The stubble in the furries—kind o' lonesome-like,

When the Frost Is on the Punkin *(cont.)*

R4: but still a-preachin' sermuns to us of the barns they growed to fill;

R5: The strawstack in the medder,

R6: and the reaper in the shed;

R1: The hosses in theyr stalls below—

R2: the clover overhead!—

R3: O, it sets my hart a-clickin' like the tickin' of a clock,

ALL: When the frost is on the punkin and the fodder's in the shock.

R4: Then your apples all is gethered,

R5: and the ones a feller keeps is poured around the cellar-floor in red and yaller heaps;

R6: And your cider-makin's over,

R1: and your wimmern-folks is through with theyr mince and apple-butter,

R2: and theyr souse and sausage too! . . .

R3: I don't know how to tell it—

R4: but ef such a thing could be as the angels wantin' boardin',

R5: and they'd call around on me—

R6: I'd want to 'commodate 'em-all the whole-indurin' flock—

ALL: When the frost is on the punkin and the fodder's in the shock.

NOTE: This is a difficult script because of Riley's Hoosier dialect of the Midwest region. My class in 5th grade was likely successful with it because we spent a few days in class just doing the entire poem to a steady rhythm. Although I usually shy away from rhyme in scripts for the upper grades, this one has the whimsy of a tongue twister. Beginning slowly and then quickening the steady beat, helped the children to increase fluency on a very challenging poem. This script has become a class favorite.

The Christmas Pudding

Illustrated London News (December, 1848)

A Reader's Theater for 3 voices

R1: In a household where there are five or six children, the eldest not above ten or eleven, the making of the pudding is indeed an event.

R2: It is thought of days, if not weeks, before.

R3: To be allowed to share in the noble work, is a prize for young ambition. . .

ALL: Lo!

R1: the lid is raised,

R2: curiosity stands on tip-toe,

R3: eyes sparkle with anticipation,

R2: little hands are clapped in ecstasy,

R1: almost too great to find expression in words.

ALL: The hour arrives-the moment wished and feared;

R2 & 3: wished, oh! how intensely;

R1: feared, not in the event, but lest envious fate should not allow it to be an event, and mar the glorious concoction in its very birth.

ALL: And then when it is dished,

R3: when all fears of this kind are over,

R2: when the roast beef has been removed,

R1: when the pudding, in all the glory of its own splendour, shines upon the table,

ALL: how eager is the anticipation of the near delight!

R1: How beautifully it steams!

R2: How delicious it smells!

R3: How round it is!

R1: A kiss is round,

R2: the horizon is round,

R3: the earth is round,

R1: the moon is round,

R2 & 3: the sun and stars, and all the host of heaven are round.

R1, 2 & 3: So is plum pudding.

NOTE: This is a higher reading level, only because the content would probably be understood more deeply by the older students. This script would embellish a study on English Christmas tradition, Dickens, or "Twas the Night Before Christmas." My students have struggled to believe that simply pulling a plum pudding out of the oven could be such an exciting event. A friend of mine, whose father is English, says that this script taken from an old English newspaper is not an exaggeration of the excitement surrounding the event!

The Ant and the Chrysalis

A Reader's Theater for 4 voices: Narrators 1 and 2, Butterfly, Ant

Narrator 1: An Ant nimbly running about in the sunshine in search of food came across a Chrysalis that was very near its time of metamorphosis.

Narrator 2: The Chrysalis moved its tail, and attracted the attention of the Ant, who then saw for the first time that it was alive.

Ant: Poor, pitiful animal! What a sad fate is yours! While I can run hither and thither, at my pleasure, and, if I wish, ascend the tallest tree, you lie imprisoned here in your shell, with power only to move a joint or two of your scaly tail.

N2: The Chrysalis heard all this, but did not try to make any reply.

N1: A few days after, when the Ant passed that way again, nothing but the shell remained.

N2: Wondering what had happened to its contents, the ant felt himself suddenly shaded and fanned by the gorgeous wings of a beautiful Butterfly.

Butterfly: Behold in me, your much-pitied friend! Boast now of your powers to run and climb! But it will be difficult to get me to listen.

N1: After he said this, the Butterfly rose in the air, and, borne along and aloft on the summer breeze, was soon lost to the sight of the Ant forever.

All: The moral of this fable is "Appearances are deceptive."

Index